To Terry

Thoughts for
a New Perspective

Many Blessings,
Thanks for your friendship

Kurt Dol

THOUGHTS FOR
A NEW PERSPECTIVE

Kurt M. Jordan

THOUGHTS FOR A NEW PERSPECTIVE

iUniverse books may be ordered through booksellers or by contacting:

iUniverse LLC
1663 Liberty Drive
Bloomington, IN 47403
www.iuniverse.com
1-800-Authors (1-800-288-4677)

Because of the dynamic nature of the Internet, any web addresses or links contained in this book may have changed since publication and may no longer be valid. The views expressed in this work are solely those of the author and do not necessarily reflect the views of the publisher, and the publisher hereby disclaims any responsibility for them.

Any people depicted in stock imagery provided by Thinkstock are models, and such images are being used for illustrative purposes only. Certain stock imagery © Thinkstock.

ISBN: 978-1-4917-4059-0 (sc)
ISBN: 978-1-4917-4058-3 (e)

Library of Congress Control Number: 2014912183

Printed in the United States of America.

iUniverse rev. date: 07/29/2014

For the Higher Self within Humanity

CONTENTS

PREFACE

Writing *Thoughts for a New Perspective* arose from a desire to expand human consciousness by initiating a transformative conversation one thought at a time. Too often we see only what we're conditioned to see, whether by our parents, environment, education, religious beliefs, mass media, or society in general. These narrow-minded perspectives can limit our growth to a type of tunnel-vision existence that tends to separate us rather than unite us, and bind us rather than free us. If these thoughts can help remove the blinders surrounding human consciousness, the result will be a new perspective.

INTRODUCTION

In such a crazy world, do you find yourself saying, "I don't know what to think anymore"? Are you clueless about what you can do about it? Would you like to experience a fresh outlook on life, gain new insights, and explore other points of view? Within these pages you will discover many different ways to think about God, interesting questions to ask about life, and thoughts about relationships, wisdom, love and spirit a virtual smorgasbord of contemporary thoughts needed for a new perspective. *Thoughts for a New Perspective* delivers an internal dialogue that reaches deep into the soul and spirit, while engaging and stimulating the mind. These thoughts resonate with your frequency, integrating a vibration in consciousness that opens your eyes to perceive other possible ways of thinking. It's like using the delete button on your computer; what stays or goes is up to you. Remember, thought is primal energy that we use to create and re-create our lives, while our words and deeds are always secondary manifestations of our thinking. We know the saying: change your thoughts, change your life. So give yourself and others the gift of something new to think and talk about for the next one hundred years of being human and divine.

Chapter 1

~ GOD ~

The original creator, the Supreme Being, life itself, self-existing one that is in the creation and yet is beyond creation; the love of the universe, the source of the all in all, which stands eternal; infinite universal intelligence unaffected by time or space, ageless and all powerful transcending the comprehension of limited minds, the is that is, the I Am that I Am, the light, thought, mind and the word able to manifest anything finding nothing too hard or impossible to do except lie, unconditionally loving, the truth that upholds all things, ever-expanding awesomeness, unmovable, unshakeable, unstoppable, beyond description and indefinable.

* * The Meeting * *

"God, what an honor it is to meet you."

Beyond Science

The only one to do a successful heart transplant without anesthesia, scalpel, or drugs is God, by performing the miracle of a changed heart.

A Gift from God

Forgiveness is a gift from God for us to give to ourselves and others.

Equal = Equal

All men and women are created equal in the sight of God. Yet men and women are not treated equally. God leaves that up to us. Why do we know that we are equal in every respect yet deny it in every respect? Nobody is better than anybody else. Flesh and bone, blood, the body of humanity is the body of equality acting out inequality. When will we ever learn that inequality never works? When will we see the mathematics of humanity in the same way that we see that $1 + 5 = 6$, and $2 + 4 = 6$, and $1 + 1 + 1 + 1 + 1 = 1 = 6$, or $8 - 2 = 6$? Figures don't lie, but liars figure that some are not equal with others, that some people count while others do not. The truth is that we all count the same; the sum of our parts is equal to the whole.

Write God, Right

You need to get in touch with God, right? Grab a pen and paper and write God a letter, write what you feel; say what you mean, and mean what you say. If you live alone, leave it on the kitchen table or the bed, anywhere you want to. If not, put it where only God will find it. If you don't think God will find it, tell God where you put it, right? Then head off to work, right? When you get home, thank God for reading your letter, right? Ask, *Dear God, what did you think about my letter*? Write God. Right!

Are You Running on Empty?

We are living in the day where you can have all that you want and still feel empty. If you are running on empty, only God can fulfill you.

The Whole Individual

Though I am individualized, I am a part of the whole. Therefore, I am whole, though I am individualized as a part.

No Fear

How much fear is too much fear? The answer is that any fear is too much fear. "Fear not," saith God, "for I am with thee." Fear binds our potential, paralyzes our dreams, and keeps us small. God frees our potential, sets dreams in motion, and keeps us growing bigger.

Reconnected or Disconnected?

Those who are disconnected from God-mindedness keep others disconnected. Those who are connected to God-mindedness seek to help others become reconnected.

I Wonder Why

I wonder why God has allowed the truth and religious confusion to get all messed up and mixed up together. It seems like it does not bother God. I have read that you can do nothing against the truth but only for the truth. The truth behind all things simply is the truth that is God, not religious ideas about the truth that is God. In some respects we have traveled far, while in other respects we have not traveled far enough. It is time for us to travel from religiosity about God to reality that is God.

Unseeing Is Believing

Our thoughts are unseen, air is unseen, sound is unseen, smell is unseen, taste is unseen, and sensation is unseen, yet we believe in them all. We can see the creation but not the Creator, and yet many claim that they would believe if they could only see their Creator. The Creator is the substance of all creation.

The Death Killer

Bringing death to death that we may live and never die! The Christ!

The Learner's Prayer

Dear Life, may I learn more today than I did yesterday, that I may know more today than I did yesterday. And apply what I have learned today tomorrow.

Beautiful Means You!

You are a God good person who lives the God good life. Everything the good God made was good and beautiful. You were made so bea-u-tiful that God decided to insert you (as u) in the word *beautiful*. So be a you ti full good person like God!

Unconditional Love

The only condition of unconditional love is that it be unconditional. We all like to think we love unconditionally, and it is great when we do. God loves us with this kind of love. Sometimes we hear people say if God loves us unconditionally, how could he let their lives get in so bad a condition. How can bad things happen to innocent people? God loves you in spite of your condition and bad things that happen; therein lies unconditional love.

R.I.P.

I am the peace of God because I am a piece of God on the earth. The peace that lasts becomes peace at last; therefore, resting in peace is for the living, not the dead. One can find rest in peace, and peace in one's rest, when one remembers that one is a piece of God.

Does God Exist?

Those who sleep dream that there is no God, and the dream becomes a nightmare. Unbearable as it is, they dream on in this way. One day the dream will end, as we awaken to the truth and love of God. At that time questions and debates about God will end. And all will agree it was a very bad dream that seemed so real. We called it life without God—an absolutely impossibility, for God is.

A Great Secret

I have learned a great secret today. Therefore, it is no longer a secret to me. However, it is great. It has to do with returning to "oneness." Separate yourself only from the thought/belief of separation. Oneness will be the result.

Salvation

Everyone wants to be saved; they just do not have understanding of the truth concerning salvation.

Let Us Do It!

We came here to master love and forgiveness, to experience oneness again with God and one another. We can do it, so let's do it!

Spiritual

I understand but a few things, but the few shall become many, and through Christ, the many shall become all.

God's Children

The greatest prayer is to pray for God's children, and who of us is not?

Ancestors

We are the physical extensions of our ancestors, and we are the spiritual extensions of the living spirit of God, the ancient eternal creator.

Hurt Not

I shall not hurt God's children.

Loving God

If you love God your life will be much happier.

Eye Candy

Fake fulfillment is not fulfillment at all. One must learn to distinguish between the temporal candy and that which is eternal. Eye candy is sweet, colorful, and delightful to eat, but it soon dissolves into nothing. Where does eternal sweetness abide but with God, the source?

Higher-Frequency Thoughts

Only God can open your eyes; human perception is subject to error.

What If?

What if you were rich but did not know it? Would you not live in poverty? What if you were love but did not know it? Would you not suffer also? What if you were light but didn't know it? Would you not stumble in darkness? The truth is that you are the rich, loving light. We breathe the breath of life; without it we fall down and perish. Yet if we have not money, sex, power, or purpose, we stand to live another day. It is the inhale and the exhale that is primary. All else is secondary. Moreover, God breathed the breath of life into humanity, and we became living souls. God comes first, then life.

The Absolute Desire

There are many desires one can have, the main one being the desire for absolute truth, for absolute truth will never change. God is love and truth, and love and truth is the absolute desire.

Goodness

God is the goodness we all desire in our lives, we think that we can find the goodness we desire without God, a grave and unfortunate thought. God is the source of all the good. The word *good is complimentary to God.* "Good = God."

Wise Request

Help me do your will; then what I do will not be in vain.

Awesome Thought!

Do you see yourself as a part of God or apart from God?

Since God Sense

Since the only thing that makes any sense in my life right now is God, I can find no sense in the world.

God's Thoughts

We all become our thoughts. They shape our behaviors, they mold our personalities, and they even create our destinies or send us to our fates.

To become the thoughts of God is the ultimate in oneness of individual expression, for it is God expressing in you as you through divine thoughts. The following is from the book of Isaiah, chapter 55, verses 8 and 9: KJV "For my thoughts are not your thoughts, nor are your ways my ways, saith God. For as the heavens are higher than the earth, so are my ways higher than your ways, and my thoughts than your thoughts."

Playing with God

Those who play with God have found the joy of playing with God. Can you imagine actually playing with God?

One Being One

In being one, do I not draw unto myself that which is my own?

Heartbeat!

How many of us live with shrapnel in our hearts, emotional injuries sustained from the darkest days of our lives? From the outside we seem whole, unscarred, even smiling when asked, "How are you?" We reply, "I'm fine." Yet underneath beat hearts full of shrapnel. There is an encouraging Scripture in the Bible that tells us God will heal the brokenhearted. I believe it is an invitation for us to give our broken hearts to God.

One with God

There is power in being one with God.

Don't Believe in God?

If you don't believe in God ...God believes in you. So you might as well give up your unbelief.

Under Pressure

There is no pressure from God. Any pressure you feel is simply your own futile resistance.

God Loves Me Too

When you hear someone say, "God loves you," do you say, "I love me too?" If you do not love yourself, you disagree with God's love. When you agree with God's love, you are in alignment with love. The next time someone says they love you, say, "I love me too" (with a smile). Look at their face and see what they do. If they start to act funny, say, "Evidently you agree with God, and I do too."

God-Given Potential

Each of us has the potential of living a better life when our hearts are open. In hospitals we find people in need of open-heart surgery to save their lives. Yet is it not those with closed hearts that need open-heart surgery? It is our self-mindedness that determines which way our hearts shall be. God has given us a heart that includes others; and when we exclude others, we exclude ourselves from sharing in the great heart of love. God is the great love that supports and strengthens us to open our hearts the more. It is God's will for humanity to have a open hearts, for only in this will we ever have peace. Remember the cry of the human heart is "Please love me forever!"

The Sparrow

Perhaps the reason God knows if a sparrow falls to the ground is that God is the sparrow's life expression. God is not watching every sparrow; God *is* every sparrow. How much more valuable are you to God than is a sparrow? The sparrow does not worry, so why should we? Perhaps the sparrow knows what we choose to deny.

Prayer Time

What if the dominate thoughts and feelings that we consistently believe about ourselves and others is also prayer time?

A Prayer Thought

The greatest prayer that can be prayed is by the Christ self within; such a prayer cannot go unanswered.

Low versus High

How often we attempt to invite God into our lower-consciousness thinking instead of accepting God's invitation to higher-consciousness thinking? We can overcome our lower false nature by the higher true nature.

The Architect of Man

One day while at work I entered the blueprint room, looking for a blueprint that showed how a certain doorway was constructed. I never did find it; however, I went through many a print of this 1931 historical landmark building. Each print showed the exact dimensions and materials used in the making of the building. The blueprints came from the architect, when there was no building except in his mind. We have life. Surely there is a master blueprint for our lives, and surely there is an architect greater than us who has an image of us in his great mind. For just as a building cannot be made without a blueprint, neither can we just happen to be so beautiful.

"Oh, My God" Thought!

Oh, my God! Oh, my God! Check it out. Years ago a guy had a bag of marijuana sitting on his truck's dashboard. He was traveling down the highway, rolling a joint, when suddenly the wind blew the bag right out the window. He exclaimed, "Oh, my God!" And then he began to think about what he said as he went back to find that bag.

* * *One Bottom Line* * *

I am one with the One.

Thanks, God

I came before God not asking for anything. I thanked God instead, for everything. If you want to make God smile, this is how you can do it. Find a quiet space of time and say, "I come before you, God, not to ask for anything but to thank you for everything."

The Search Is Over

Our lives are full of searching; we search for love, friends, wealth, acceptance, truth, answers, prestige, respect, peace, power, healing, and feeling. They who search for immortality are few. They shall eventually find it, for it is the destiny of humanity to return unto the immortal, indestructible, incorruptible life that is in the mind of God. And in that instant they shall say, "God is more awesome than I thought."

Camouflaged

What about God in disguise? Could you recognize God?

* * God Is * *

God is the life of the believer; God is the life of the unbeliever.

Reflecting Oneness

We are a reflection of the One. Look into a mirror; you are both places at once. Everything is a reflection of the One. Humanity appears divided yet we are a reflection of oneness extending out from God.

Know God

Acknowledge God as the mighty "I Am" presence in yourself as well as in all things.

God Never ...

God never meant us to be lonely, broke, sick, unfulfilled, frustrated, angry, depressed, or suicidal. Though we may be these things more often than not, that was never intended.

Signed Sealed Delivered

I'm yours.

High Self/God Self

We can always go to our higher self, who is just waiting to be acknowledged and expressed. Since we have access to our God self and can always go there, we might as well go there and practice staying there.

You Remind Me of ...

May I be something or someone who reminds you of God, and may you always remind me of God.

Sameness

I love the light, the light I love; I am the light, and the light I am.

Hell, You're Fired!

Hellfire and eternal damnation or love eternal and reconciliation? Come on, which one makes sense? Which one speaks to your heart and not your head?

All or Nothing

With God all things are possible; without God nothing is possible. Seeing all the possibilities that have manifested, we can conclude that it is all possible and that there is nothing impossible with God. Are you with God on this?

The Homecoming

What is the pay-off in forgiveness? We get to come home, and there is no place like home. God said, "Forgive everyone and come home." You see, homecoming is not the act of dying; on the contrary, it is coming into life, getting beyond illusions, retuning and returning to love, which is of course the source we know as God. In this way, with love in our hearts, we experience the homecoming.

God

I like God!

~ *God's Poetry* ~

If we think we cannot pray, perhaps send us out to sea, and if we should survive we'll know why we're alive, a prayer we prayed with all our heart more times than we could count, when all has gone seemingly wrong with little hope in sight there lies within our heart a little glimmer of light, though all is dark and distant too, that shred of hope we do cling to, with faith we claimed we didn't have. We dare not toss faith overboard our hope would sure be dashed. If just one miracle far and few would light upon the heart and give that little glimmer of hope a bright and brand new start. But time will tell if we're holding on in vain, for we know without a miracle from God our hope will surely wane. Until there's nothing left to see, nothing left to be, I think we'll learn to talk with God without going out to sea.

Chapter 2

~ QUESTIONS ~

To question something indicates a desire to know the truth. The truth is the only answer to the question. What is the first question? Have I not asked it and answered it?

Dreams and Nightmares

How many people are living their dreams, and how many are living their nightmares? When you are living the dream and invite others, they get to experience your joyful dream. When you are living in your nightmare, everyone is trying to escape sheer terror, including you.

Lifetime

Tick-tick goes the clock of our lives. No sooner than we arrive, we depart, not knowing whence we came or where we are going. All we know is that we are here for a time. We count the time; the clock repeats itself repeatedly, again it is 12 a.m., 12 p.m., 12 a.m., and 12 pm. Yet the clock of our lives is quite different. We are five years old only once. There seems to be a time of events. The clock is ticking. What are you doing with the time of your life?

Feeling No Pain!

Have you ever heard someone say that he or she isn't feeling any pain, because they are so drunk? Feeling no pain is actually feeling the pain. That is why they are drunk: the pain of an unfulfilled life with more questions than they have answers.

Mirror, Mirror

When is the last time you gave yourself a smile? When you look in the mirror, do you frown, scream, cry, or look down? Do you look past the person looking back at you, do you ignore yourself, do you see your dearest friend, or do you see your worst enemy? When is the last time you gave yourself a smile in the mirror, mirror?

The Sun

Sunrise and sunset, are they not the same?

Lifetime Question

Actions are done in time. Can time exist without action? What is life without action? What is life without time? What happens if time fades away?

Two Questions

What makes one person say, "I can't stand this or that," and another person say, "It doesn't bother me in the least"? Is it the person or the thing?

Are You Aware?

When you are aware of everyone in your view, through thinking, vision, or hearing, are you aware of you?

Now Understand That

Understanding comes with understanding that understanding comes with understanding. Now understand that understanding comes with understanding that.

Are You Engaged?

No conversation is more important than the one you are currently engaged in. Let's you and I both turn our attention toward each other and disengage our technological tendency to engage in another conversation that can wait!

What Now Is It?

Is that what we're doing? Moving through the now, not time?

What Happens

We search for it, whatever it is, and when we find it, what happens?

What Is Beautiful?

What makes a person beautiful is the part of him or her that cannot be seen but, rather, wholly felt.

What's in a Name?

Take Paul Newman, for instance, who became Paul old man. When I think of Clint Eastwood, I picture him in a western. Morgan Freeman is a free man because he's a Freeman. Rachel Ray is a ray of hope for women who seek self-expression in the kitchen. How does the chairman of the board keep the board meeting from being the bored meeting? Then we have Dr. Phil, who helps people feel better. And Dr. Oz who has taken America on the wonderful wizard Oz adventure to better health. Can it be Friday on Thursday because you're frying fish that day? Should bachelors have bachelor's degree in being bachelors?

Love?

What is love is it for everyone or just for the ones you love? God so loved everyone.

What If?

What if God has plans for you that you don't know anything about? Awesome plans! Would you be interested?

Do You Agree?

If your thoughts are disagreeable, you will tend to be likewise disagreeable. We cannot be separate from our thoughts, or can we?

What a Thought

It is nice to be nice, and it is stupid to be stupid. It is wise to be wise, and it is hateful to be hateful. It is lovely to be lovely, and it is thoughtful to be thoughtful. If our thoughts are but something in the mind, conceived by an individual, as an idea, an opinion, or belief, then answer this question: What is the origin of thought? What is the origin of the idea, opinion, or belief?

Choices

A relationship is only as good as its foundation; shall we build our relationships on love, truth, equality, and respect or on hatred, lies, inequality, and disrespect?

Why Not?

Have a great day just because you deserve it!

Expectations

Acting and reacting out of other people's expectations is useless, yet we do it anyway. Is it all just an act for them or for us? Is it necessary?

Happiness

It has been said that affection in our life is nine-tenths of our happiness. If we lack affection in our lives, how do we redefine our happiness?

Unknown Thought

The question that covers the unknown is "Now what?" Could it be love?

Time to Clean House

If a clean house is a happy house, then a clean mind should be a happy mind.

Finding Good Help

Whom can I help today? What good can I do today?

Well Enough Alone

We often say to leave well enough alone, but what if it is not well enough?

Of Course

Can you become younger than you were yesterday? How about smarter? How about lovelier?

Just a Thought out of Control

Those who feel the need to control others have gone beyond the limits of self-control. I personally prefer to be out of control; it's an illusion to even think that you can be in control of anything or anyone. It is only your thoughts that you can get control of; the way you think and what thoughts you choose is the only thing under your conscious control. Yet who or what controls the consciousness?

Time to Complain

Who has time to complain about things they can do nothing about?

I would say nearly everyone.

Mirror on the Wall

When you look in the mirror, do you see the light?

Can You Answer the Question

When we tell someone to keep going, that they can make it, what if we honestly know that they can't make it? My mother said, "If God wills it, you will make it."

Could Be Right

Can I be right when it looks like I am wrong again?

Worldview

Do you see the world? How do you see it? Do you see the world through God's eyes or through blind eyes?

Just a Thought, Do Not Panic!

Since the devil is a lie and the truth is not in him, and a lie is not real (never has been and never will be), then can the devil be real, when the only thing real is the truth?

Faith without Works Is Dead

Why did you buy boat shoes? For my yacht. What yacht? You don't have a yacht! I have to start somewhere. For having yacht shoes without the yacht is aliveness.

Forward March!

Life is a forward march, so how or why do we go backward?

What People Say

I hear people say they are a day late and a dollar short. They say another day, another dollar. Then, to top it off, they say life is a bitch and then you die. I hear people describing someone as drop-dead gorgeous. Are these supposed to be positive affirmations to live by?

?

What is the question of the day? That is the question.

Alone Thought

Have you ever walked the road alone?

Eternal Thought

Life is eternal; is not the air we breathe always here?

Ironic Thought

I overheard a woman talking about the dog she and her husband kept in their home. One day she let the dog out and could not find her. In a panic she exclaimed, "He would kill me if anything happened to her! That's his baby!" Whom did he love more, his wife or his dog?

What a Question!

What person hath hated his own flesh? What person hath cursed himself? What person hath struck himself in the mouth with his own fist? Why do unto others what you would not do unto yourself?

The World

If it is not about money, what would it be about?

Again and Again

Is not tomorrow today again and again? Is not today tomorrow again and again?

Agreement

As we live our lives, there are countless things that we can disagree about, from the taste of something to a court case decision. This often results in conflict. Even wars are usually about a disagreement, and divorces are, for sure.

Perhaps before we point out what we disagree on, we should ask, "What can we agree on?" In this way we accentuate the positive. Would you agree or disagree?

I Thought about Thought

Everything made was once a thought, an idea, without form, abstract, in a nonexistent state. Things are thoughts that have manifested from the invisible dimensions of our minds. So tell me, what are thoughts made of? If the answer is consciousness, then what is consciousness?

Greatness

Have you expressed any greatness today?

Let's Face It!

Sometimes people are captured by their own image, convinced they are the biological being of illusion they see in the mirror. As the decades pass, the illusion in the mirror decays right before our very eyes. We frantically seek solutions in makeup, potions, and liposuction. We lift and tuck, spending big bucks. The truth of who we are is somehow cloaked by the illusion. We love the illusion, yet we despise it when it turns against us, never suspecting that it cannot be truth if it is an illusion. Can you face who you really are?

Boomerang Thought

If all the evil a person does comes back to them, and all of the good a person does comes back to them, what is the logical thing for you to do? Good or evil?

Genetic Manipulations

Are we under the power of a genetic manipulation over which we have no control? If I shave the hair from my arm, somehow the hair knows that it has been cut, and it grows back to a predetermined length. All this being the case that hair is supposed to be dead. The body I live in is actually a genetic compilation of my parents and their parents, going back to who knows where. Biological genetic manipulations, patterns of DNA creating bodies for us to live in.

When looking at one another we fail to see who or whatever we are because of our invisibility. It has been said that the eye is the window to the soul; therefore, when you look into my eyes, I am staring back at your genetic representation of what I call you. I am looking at you from my invisible soul, which sits in the seat of my consciousness looking through my eye, the window where I peer out at you. You should check me out sometime, and I will check you out. Can we get past the genetic manipulation, can we get past the eye, to get to the I that is me, which is you in a different genetically manipulated body?

Financial Forgiveness

There are many things for which we need to forgive ourselves; have you ever thought of financial forgiveness?

After You Awaken

Whatever you believe to be real in a dream becomes real to you, even though it's a dream and not real at all. Have you ever noticed how a dream does not seem real after you wake up?

Thoughts That Bind or Free

Thoughts can bind you, or thoughts can free you. Therein lies the great power of our thoughts. Beliefs can better you, or beliefs can beat you. What are you thinking, and what are you believing?

Can You Believe This?

Everything that Christ did as miracles pertained to the reality of the kingdom of heaven, not the illusion of the world. When he opened the eyes of the blind, unstopped the deaf ears, caused the lame to walk, and raised the dead, all of these were a symbol of humanity's spiritual condition without the light. With the light we would see the truth that sets us free, hear the words *I love you*, and walk the pathway that leads unto life. Humanity has been a dead man walking in death, which we call life. The Christ will raise us out of death into a life of living light that never dies. The same works shall we do as Christ. Can you believe this?

Give Me What You Got

You cannot give someone what you lack in yourself; if you do not have meat, you cannot give meat; if you have no money, you cannot give it. Conversely, you can give to others what you have within your possession. If you have love, you can give love; and if you have life, you can give life. Christ had, gave, and demonstrated both. What do you have to give?

A Good Question

If I can look into your eyes and see into your soul. Then you should be able to look into my eyes and see my soul. Right?

How Do You Act?

The world is a set stage, complete with actors. What will you do? What are your acts? For in the great script it shall be written, "And these were the acts of [insert your name]."

A Conscious Question?

What is consciousness? I think it is a living energy that is aware through the five sense faculties but not limited to them. To be unconscious is a type of unawareness or the inability to access conscious awareness. I think consciousness is aware of being. When a person recovers after being in a coma, they may have no conscious memory of the time they were in a coma. So where did consciousness go, and what reconnected them to it again?

Being You

How do you like being you? Do you like yourself or dislike yourself; do you hate being you or love the being you?

The Rest of My Life

When people say, "I want to spend the rest of my life with you," how can they say this unless they know the rest of their life?

Our Birthday Suit

We all are self-conscious about being seen in our birthday suit, yet everyone is a replica of the two body types: male or female. Somewhere in the mind, we feel the need to be covered. How does a stripper strip in a strip club? Where does she go in her mind? Some may say she has no shame, no self-respect, not a moral fiber left in her being. What about a small child who runs from the bedroom naked into a room of adults? Does the child have no shame, respect, or morals? Somehow the stripper has gone somewhere in her mind; has she returned to the place where a little child's mind is? Does she just block it all out, or is she devoid of self-respect? Bottom line, we are all strippers.

A Strange and Friendly Question

Are we strangers pretending to be friends, or are we friends pretending to be strangers?

A Space Thought

Am I just taking up space, or am I the space that is just being taken up?

Awareness without Thought

Have you ever experienced a moment of awareness where you find yourself staring without a single thought at all, a time where all thought seems to be suspended? You experience pure awareness, all without any thought, and then suddenly you snap out of it and start thinking thoughts again? It is a strangely peaceful experience, but not exactly a daydream. It is like a zoning out from the realm of thoughts, during which you become pure awareness.

Power Talk

A person can speak great words, but do they have great power behind them? Anyone can talk, but does anyone have anything to say?

The Flock of Faith

One day I questioned a huge flock of birds. I asked them with this thought, *How do you all find something to eat?* They replied as one: *He who made us always provides for us*, and they flew into the horizon and disappeared from my sight. This was a flock of faith-filled birds. They knew their creator and had absolute confidence that no matter how many they were, they would be provided for.

Hope

"Don't give up" indicates that there is some hope in the matter, yet if there is no hope, is it okay to give up hope?

New Day, New Thoughts

It was the month of January, the year 2003, when the following entered my consciousness, an awareness that stated, *A new day is here.* Six years later, things seemed not much changed. This is the key that turned in my mind and released this question: "Are you living in it?"

The Beauty of Me Is You

What is it that makes you beautiful to me? Is it what I see, or what I do not see? A combination of the two, perhaps. Or is it me who is reflecting my beauty onto you because I love you as I love me?

Calibration

Are you being re-calibrated for life, or are you still calibrated for death?

A Child Cries

I have observed adults with crying children. Usually tears are a genuine sign of pain, whether it is emotional, physical, or a combination of the two. The adult will say, "Quit crying," in a threatening tone of voice. I have also heard "If you don't quit crying, I'm going to give you something to cry about!" What if the child replied, "Quit crying for what? These are my tears, and I will cry if I need to; you cannot control my tears." What if a child saw his or her parent crying and said, "You better quit crying; you don't have anything to cry about"?

Hey, Baby!

You ever notice how when you are a baby everyone loves you unconditionally, you are held and kissed a lot? You grow up, get involved romantically with someone, and start calling each other "baby." You are hugged and kissed, but where is the unconditional love?

You and Others

If you cannot understand yourself, how can you understand others? As the saying goes, seek first to understand, then to be understood.

Questions and Answers

When we choose to live our lives without questions, we invariably choose to live our lives without answers. There are as many questions waiting on answers as there are answers waiting on the right questions.

Rainy Thoughts

Who is the rain; what is the rain? As it comes down to greet us, we observe it wetting everything. It saturates the earth very lightly, and at other times with a great force. It helps some people sleep better and wakes others up. The rain freshens and cleanses the air, giving us life in so many ways. It comes down and then goes up again, only to come down again on our picnics, parades, or wedding days, and we hear the bride say "Please don't... rain." Oh yes, we talk to the rain. We say, "Rain, rain, go away; please come back another day." And it does on someones special day. When it does not rain, we suffer the drought and the famine; we perish. When it rains too much, we are swept away. The river has jumped and overflowed, women and children are sinking down, Lord have mercy! We count the days since it last rained, as well as the days that it has been raining; either way our lives depend on the rain. The rain is our friend and sometimes our foe.

Time Thought

If time were to go, what would happen next?

Cloudy Question

Why do clouds sit flat in the sky when there is nothing for them to sit upon that is flat?

We Are One

What would it be like if you could meet all seven billion people on the earth? Simply look in the mirror and say "hello." We are one.

Who Won the Match?

There was a boy who wrestled, but he had no legs. Someone made the comment that it could be an advantage, because he had no legs for the other wrestler to grab. The person who was telling about the legless wrestler then replied, "No, he lost." I said, "Know he won!"

Walking upon Water

When a spiritual master is walking upon a lake, river, or ocean, do the master's feet get wet or remain dry? If they are wet, how did they walk upon it? And if they are dry, then how did they walk upon it? The only one able to answer this mystery is the one walking upon the water.

The Key to Success

I was at the BMW dealer picking up my car, which I had in for service. I opened the door and sat down, but where was the key? I looked on the dash, in the ignition, on the floor in the center console, and under the armrest. Finally I got out of the car and told them that the key was not in the car. They politely walked back to the car with me. I was confident that the key was not in the car. To my dismay, they opened the door, and there the key was, sitting on the driver's seat. They just smiled ... and I, embarrassed, blushed, smiled, and apologized. Before you blame another for why you can't get going in life, ask yourself whether you may be sitting on the key to your own success.

Thought Mastery

To master one's tongue is a great mastery, yet to master one's thoughts is truly a greater mastery. Either we gain mastery over our thoughts, or our thoughts gain mastery over us. Do you want to become a thought master?

Acting and Reacting

If all that is around us is illusion, why do we continue to act and react as though it were truth?

Full-and Part-Time

Why do people who work full-time have part-time money?

When You're Happy

When you're happy and you know it, what don't you do? Gossip, hurt yourself or others, or be unhappy.

People

We hear the things that people do that make us cringe. And we exclaim, "Oh, God, what is wrong with people?'

The answer: a lot of things.

Fear

Fear has been described as False Evidence Appearing Real. Those of us who have no fear of flying find ourselves thirty thousand feet in the sky traveling over six hundred miles an hour and yet at peace mentally and physically. What could we possibly fear when both feet are planted firmly on the ground? One thousand things and counting. Fear not, says love.

Is It?

When it all seems unreal, perhaps it all is.

A Toast

Let us make a toast to *what if?*

~ *Questionable Poetry* ~

Could you ever be true, could you ever just be you? So much to say, yet words cannot convey the things of the heart unseen as they are. No more to desire that you be desired but only now to be understood; you've become defenseless and fearless, open to acceptance or rejections to just be true, just be you, for the sun sets in all its beauty while the loveseat has no couple to hold, and you wonder why the glass of water is now empty and the breeze of summer turned cold; without life nothing has meaning or motion; is the door to the apartment closed? There are people washing their garments, the trampoline will not bounce without you, and the little girl wears no shoes.

Chapter 3

~ RELATIONSHIPS ~

A ship well built can withstand the crashing waves of the sea if the crew knows what to do in the worst of storms. The first ship that ever sailed was "The Relationship," with a crew of two called me and you, with hopes set high. We didn't know how hard the wind could blow, or how high waves would flow, until we were drenched from head to toe. When love has gone overboard, all the dreams you thought you had begin to fade like footprints in the sand. Yet not all relationships are doomed; there are successful relationships that manage the storms, challenge the waves, and live to sail on the winds of love another day. Your first relationship is the one you have with yourself. Do you like yourself, do you love who you are, do you know who you are, and can you forgive yourself, or do you judge, criticize, condemn, hate, and kill yourself? Do you have compassion for yourself; do you encourage yourself? Do you ask for divine help or do you think not? These and many other factors will determine your experiences in relationships.

Be the First

Be the first person that you hug today, that you help today, that you smile at today, and that you love today.

Relationship Advice

The first relationship we have is the one with ourselves; this tends to determine how we will relate to others in our lives. Creating a healthy and wonderful relationship with yourself will not only enrich your life but will enrich the lives of those you meet.

Safety First

In relationships we are supposed to make each other feel safe: Safe Always From Everything.

To Be

If we are going to be something to someone, we should be their dream and not their worst nightmare.

The Law of Allowing

We allow people to flow into our lives; we allow people to flow out also. It's the natural flow of life.

The Law of the Ass

Sometimes I hear men say, "I'm getting that ass." The law of the ass states that you can get only that which you are, and that is all that you get. An ass for an ass.

Here's to Missing You

To miss someone can be a bummer, to love the one you miss, you will discover. Keep on loving, and you will recover when you find that loving is never a bummer.

The Pleasure of You

There are many pleasures in life, and you are definitely one of them. Remember this.

Celebrating Me

For the love of me and God as one, I celebrate the continuity of my life, with its ups and downs, failures and successes, the ugly and the beautiful. I honor it all, the stupidity and the brilliance of me, the flesh and the spirit you see, the unique expression I call celebrating me.

To Have and to Hold

It is better to have warmth to hold than to have not and feel the cold.

* * Earth Jewels * *

Women are the jewels of the earth.

Deletable

We have become so deletable, with our e-mail and our text messaging, our ignore button and our dismiss key.

Romantic and Row woman tic

To awake with you lying next to me, feeling the warmth of your heart and the familiarity of your kiss is bliss. What makes a man tic is what makes a woman tic, we call romantic.

Passion Time

There is always time for love if we will take the time to love and enjoy aliveness with passion. To live and be passionately in love is passion time.

Wives and Husbands

Love is the coupler that makes them a couple, marriage is the union, the connectivity that their bodies need, that their spirits, minds, and souls seek to find individual expression as one, wherein they become energetically fused together as husbands and wives.

Eye I Eye

Beauty is in the I of the beholder, and "I am going to be holding you close to me," says the eye of the beholder.

The Fish Scream

When my cousin Leona goes fishing, she hates to hear the fish scream when they're caught, so she releases them. Yet we do not hear the scream that our cruel and callous words cause others. Our insensitivity and indifference stab the soul, crush the spirit, and dismember the heart. When we carelessly cast our words about like extra-sharp barbed hooks, they leave unseen damages within.

Making Love

When God made you, God must have been thinking of me. How blessed you and I are, making love our eternal habitation, pressed together as one.

Choices

A relationship is only as good as its foundation; shall we build our relationships on love, truth, equality, and respect or on hatred, lies, inequality, and disrespect?

We

Is it you or is it me? There is no you without me, and there is no me without you. It is about humanity, known as we.

Being One

If you are going to love, you are going to forgive; and if you are going to forgive, you are going to love. If you are not going to forgive, you are not going to love. Love is for giving. Love and forgiveness is the marriage made in heaven. Together they can deal with any situation successfully.

Home and Heart

One's home should exhibit symbols of love and togetherness, for home is where the heart is.

True Love Agreement

A woman once said to a man, "We don't have to agree on anything to love each other." I agree!

Self-Forgiven

Find out how many people you can forgive today by starting with the one in the mirror.

Hearing Silence

It's the little sounds that we hear that make us more attentive. From the loud sounds we shield our hearing. Silence is golden and you are golden, my dear, yet I hope to hear from you soon.

The Secret Wish

When a person hates you, it is their secret wish for you to become like them. When a person loves you, it is their secret wish for you to become like them.

The Couple

Couples coupled become uncoupled couples, who seek to be coupled again.

Affection

The kiss that left me speechless showed me the power of affection.

Without You

I love you completely, profoundly, and dearly. Without you I am like …a bird missing a wing.

Count the Cost!

I can always afford to love you, for it costs me nothing; yet if I cannot afford to love you, it will cost me everything.

Facing Happiness and Joy

When I see your face, I am filled with happiness, and when I hear your voice, I am filled with joy. When I see your face, I am faced with happiness and joy.

Are You Dying to Have Sex?

"If you love yourself, protect yourself," an African musician sings about the disastrous AIDS epidemic. Currently 7,500 are infected daily with this very preventable virus. Thirty-two million have died, and the numbers are rising. That which once brought only life is bringing death also.

An Unfaithful Thought

It is the adulterous thought that leads to the adultery.

Reunions

Mini-reunions are better than none at all; family does matter.

The Meaning of Mankind

Consider mankind: man + kind = men should be kind. Consider the same with womankind: woman + kind = women should be kind also.

Feel the Need

After you feel someone's need, you can fill someone's need.

Being Free

To look past a person's fear and defensive position is to see them as they are, crouching in a corner of their frightened mind. How do I do this? By first living in the light, being free of fear and defensiveness within myself.

Sexy

If I want you for one night, I don't want you for my life; you are beyond sex, see! Before sexy ... love, beyond sexy ... love, before sexy ... love.

Never and Always

Never take out your unhappiness upon others, but always take out your happiness upon others.

Trusting You

You mean something to me; I want you to know that I trust you.

Anytime

Anytime you can place your hand in mine, anytime.

Togetherness

People in relationships sometimes part; they often say they have changed over the course of the relationship. We should go in with this mind-set, change together, and stay together.

Sometimes

Sometimes the words we do not say speak louder and clearer than the words we do say.

Soul Mates

We should treat our soul mate better than the sole mate of our shoe; for when we do there is nothing that two souls cannot walk through.

Some Thoughts about Abuse and Divorce

One day a friend and I were in a discussion about why spouses separate and divorce. My friend felt that men get tired of the same wife. I challenged his assumption with this observation. The Bible states that husbands shall love their wives as they love themselves, and no man hates his own flesh, for the two become as one in the marriage. So my question to him was, Does a man get tired of himself? He answered no. I asked then how that could be true. The bottom line, if you love yourself, then love herself, if when you look in the mirror you are all right with you, then when you look at her, don't say I'm tired of her and start looking for someone new, for if you do, you may become tired again. Furthermore, what man has ever punched himself in the mouth, or cursed himself out?

Beautiful Things

I enjoy the beautiful things in life, of which you are one.

Painful Relationships

No one is interested in another episode of crash and burn. Yet some continue to crash and burn.

It's Over

When it's over, you have to get over that it's over. Then it's over.

Kissing, Hugging, and Holding Hands

I think when we are in a relationship with another that we subconsciously try to make the person remember the feeling that they felt as a little child. That loving affection and attention was given without anything expected in return; we were loved so well just as we were. We call each other "baby." Let me kiss my baby; keep on hugging me, baby; let me hold your hand, baby. Let me love you, baby.

The Tulips

A departing lover is like a hummingbird that, after sucking on your two lips, goes looking for more tulips. It is like a butterfly that is faithful to not one flower but flies happily to the next flower.

Erase Her

Erase her from my heart; I need a brand-new start. With a kiss she wrote her name upon my heart; it's time I erase her from my heart.

Being Perfect

I do not need perfect skin, teeth, clothes, house, family, or whatever to be perfectly me.

Acting Lessons

We all are acting even when we say we are not. Acting as a friend, as a boss—it is all an act that we call life.

The Way to Equality

The only way that we can be equal is when we treat one another with equality.

Happiness

Why base your happiness in another when you can base it in yourself and then share it with another?

Love Relationships

I am in a relationship with love … would you care to join me?

Trust or Rust

A relationship without trust will be eaten away by rust.

Life Values

The value of life is having great relationships. You have what you keep, so value and keep what you have.

I Agree

Just because I disagree with you does not mean that I disagree of you.

Eagle Wings

Perhaps each of us has been in search of the other wing ... seeing as it takes two wings for an eagle to soar.

The Value of Perception

As long as people think that they have someone of value, they tend to stay together. But once that perception of value changes, kicked to the curb they go.

Elevate Yourself

When you use racial slurs or make other derogatory remarks against others, it is simply a futile attempt to elevate yourself by lowering another below your own low state of being. If you truly desire to elevate yourself, you must start by elevating others.

Love Forever Love

The man said, "This is my wife." I asked, "For how long?" He said, "What do you mean, how long? Forever!" "Okay. Define forever." The man became silent. Nothing is really yours forever, now is it? However, while she is in your life, show her only love. And love will show you forever!

~ *Relationship's Poetry* ~

I won't abuse you or mistreat you; I will protect you not neglect you. I will support you and not scorn you; I'll be firm but gentle toward you, I won't curse you but bless you; my prayer goes up for you. I'll teach you, not preach to you, I'll whisper and not shout at you, turn toward you and not away from you. I'll make you feel good even when you feel bad, keep you happy not sad, be your best friend and not your dad, be your warm tender lover under cover, be sweet but never smother, be respectful like you my mother, be your comfort and not another's, be your sun on cloudy days, warm your heart right from the start, make you laugh like you're taking a bubble bath. To see you smile I'll go the extra mile.

Chapter 4

~ WISDOM ~

What can we say about wisdom but that it is the envy of fools? It was with the creator in the beginning, to design the ecosystem, the web of life, the soil, the foliage, mountains, rivers, animals, and an endless variety of life that works with absolute perfection. Present-day humanity, with its industrial age, has strained this delicate web of life to its breaking point. With such an insatiable appetite for more resources and land, resulting in more rapid deforestation of our planet, where do we expect to be a hundred years from now? We still have poachers illegally killing thousands of elephants for their ivory tusks, while the rhinoceros is hunted for its horn. If this foolishness continues, we will witness an atrocity against nature, the extinction of species. We have entered the technological age with the same disregard we showed in the industrial age. We lack wisdom, and we know not what to do with the exhaust of our foolish ignorance.

Life Is Beautiful

Life is beautiful, and you have it, which makes you beautiful for life.

Purpose

When one's purpose is clear, one's mission has begun.

Best Value

It is of more value to do one's best than to try to be the best. Yet if one desires to be the best, one should always do one's best.

Now Speak

Search for the truth, know the facts, and then speak; otherwise, say nothing.

Building Character

Never miss a chance to build your character; you are the master architect, for there is nothing greater in life to build.

Lack Wisdom? Ask!

Wisdom will tell you what the lack thereof will not; one cannot lose when using wisdom. But one must have the wisdom to ask.

Body Talk

When we realize we are not our body per se, that the body is our servant, we are the master that treats the servant well, and the servant treats the master well by doing everything in its power to keep the master alive. The master does all it can to keep the servant alive. Servants are not known to abuse their masters; however, masters often abuse their humble servants.

Insight

Great insights are most often out of sight.

Fulfillment

There is nothing in this world that can bring you fulfillment. Fulfillment is within you. You can have all that is in the world, yet it was never meant to bring fulfillment, because it cannot. Fulfillment is knowing and accepting this.

When You Know Greatness

When you know that you have become a great man or woman, there is no time to stand around saying, "Look at my greatness!" That is not greatness at all. The key is sharing your greatness by helping to inspire the greatness in others.

Conundrum

Try not to use *cannot* as much as you can. And use *cannot* as much as you can, to say you *cannot* use *cannot* so that you can accomplish what you can.

Living Your Daydream

Every day not living your dream is another day not fully lived.

Life's Lemon

We are trying to squeeze meaning and purpose out of our experiences. We try repeating good memories. We try to maintain our agreeable lifestyle; we try to distance ourselves from those experiences that hurt or deprive us of the goodness of life.

Nice Vehicle!

We are the outgrowth of an idea, something grander than the sum of our individual parts. We are a conscious embodiment of something greater than flesh and blood. We simply are leasing our bodies. We cannot buy them, for they remain priceless. We are part of the consciousness that seeks to reunite with the supreme consciousness of all creation. Just as we are not the vehicle we drive, we are the consciousness that drives the vehicle. It is not what you drive that matters but what is driving you.

Your Self-Worth

You need to remind yourself that you are worth more than all the money you could ever work for. Did you know that you are worth more than nine hundred trillion dollars? There is only one of you on the whole planet; making you uniquely rare and of enormous value. Now say it! I am worth over nine hundred trillion dollars, because I am priceless! Say it over and over until you connect with that reality, and then know that you're not alone.

Be Exceptional

Consider yourself blessed when you meet an exceptional person in life, and if you have never been blessed to meet such a person, why don't you become an exceptional person, so that when people meet you, they will be exceptionally blessed?

Touch My Heart

The heart is the most important part of the body, and everybody wants to touch somebody. If you cannot touch the heart, you don't need to touch anybody.

Egoless Eagles

The ego is a weighty thing to carry; we cannot soar like eagles when we are gravitating toward the ego.

The Beauty of the Meal

The rabbit says to the eagle, I will be your meal; catch me, and it's a deal. My flesh is tasty, my blood is sweet. I give it my all to keep my own meat. With talons of steel and speed unsurpassed, this rabbit can't escape and has run its last. The beauty of the meal is the beauty of the kill. The rabbit has become the eagle's fuel, and it's a beautiful deal.

The Moment Is Now

These are the times of the moment of now. And now is the moment that you have the time. So live in the moment called now.

Talk Radio, Listen Radio

Why do we like to talk? Why do we like to listen? To talk is to give, while to listen is to receive. I think we are mimicking the universal law of reciprocity. Giving and receiving unconsciously, we obey.

Sitting Down

When we sit in a chair that is uncomfortable, we instinctively and immediately get up and look for a better place to sit down. We refuse to sit in a chair that wobbles or has a spring that pokes us in the rump. Why, then, do we so often settle for living uncomfortable lives? If you are not willing to sit in an uncomfortable chair, then why settle for living an uncomfortable life?

Good Luck

There are people who believe in luck and there are those who don't. The dictionary says: luck is a force that brings good fortune to prosper or succeed, especially by chance. I believe in luck like this: Love, Understanding, Compassion, and Kindness. I wish you luck!

Fur for Her and Skin for Him

We take another's skin just to cover our own. We think nothing of another's life. We like our furry fashions to keep our egos warm. Leather and furs, belts and briefcases, boots and handbags, billfolds and jackets—an animal's life has been jacked with.

Insanity/Mental Trash

Insane thoughts will lead to insane actions such as we see on the news. We all are responsible for what we allow to go on in the secret labyrinth of our minds. Remember, our minds are not garbage cans, nor are they a place for others to dispose of their trash. My grandmother used to say, "If you play with trash, it will get in your eye." I say if we allow trash to go in, only trash can come out. We both are right!

A Place to Forgive

Perhaps we should find a place to forgive the blind person who stepped on our foot, who broke our vase into pieces; perhaps we should find a place to forgive that person who cannot hear what we are saying, even if that person happens to be us. Forgiveness is not always so quick to forgive. Forgiveness can sometimes become a journey that we find ourselves on, with a destination known as peace, because we forgave.

Faith

We have to have faith in faith.

For Better or Worse

Either you help people become something better, or you help people become something worse.

Know Peace

There is no peace in the world, because there is no peace in the people who make up the world.

Lies and Truth

One should not preach or teach a lie and call it truth. Lies are not real; therefore, they cannot be truth. There cannot be a false truth; neither can there be a real lie.

Can

Can do can do; what can't do cannot do. So keep telling yourself that you can do what ever you believe you can do.

A Peaceful Conflict?

The source of conflict is disagreement, so why place yourself in its arena? Just go somewhere peaceful.

Healthy and Wealthy

It pays to be healthy; it costs too much to be sick. Therefore, it's better to be healthy, which is wealthy, than to be sick and go broke trying to be healthy again.

The Fortune Cookie

One afternoon while having lunch, a coworker opened his fortune cookie, only to discover that the cookie was empty; it didn't have a fortune in it. He said, "What am I supposed to do without a fortune?" I replied, "Write your own!"

Is

All observation is about oneself.

Peace

Peace comes from nonjudgment.

Puzzle of Life

A piece of a puzzle is but a piece of understanding, not the whole picture; one must know this in order for the piece to fit in the right place. If you place the pieces of the puzzle in the wrong place, the picture makes no sense. So it is with misunderstanding the puzzle of life.

Winning!

The way to win any and every argument is simple: do not participate.

Great Mastery

To master one's tongue is a great mastery, yet to master one's thoughts is a truly greater mastery.

You

When you attack, you also invite attack.

To Express Oneness

We have not known how to express oneness; we have only known and shown how to express conflict and separation. When we know our oneness, separation and conflict will cease to exist in our world, our lives, and our relationships.

Hide and Seek

When your life makes no sense, you do things that make no sense; hiding from meaning and purpose makes no sense. The only thing that makes sense is to find the meaning and purpose of life. Seek and you shall find. Knock and it shall be opened unto you.

No Threat

One should not feel threatened by another person's belief unless they are unsure of their own.

Fatherly Advice

Never be on the side of injustice and corruption. Good advice given from an African father to his young son.

Crazy Life

If your life gets crazy, do not do anything crazy. When your life seems out of control, take control of your thoughts first, seek expert advice, listen to sound counsel, make a positive choice, stick with it, and stay the course.

Real Eyes It!

Expectation to realization, yes! Now tell me what you are going to realize into your life. When you realize something, you will see it with your real eyes. It's all about first sight, which is your imagination, and then bringing it to open manifestation, which is your second sight. Expect only the best and realize it!

Flex

Learn to be flexible; it keeps you from breaking.

Something New Will Do

The constant need for something new, for more, is fueled by our unconscious desire to be complete. However, it never works. The more new things one gets is all fine but the feeling of completeness is still absent.

The Big Picture

See the bigger picture. It includes others, while the little picture includes only you.

So Much, So Little

I have very little to say, not because I know so much, but because I know so little about so much.

Trouble

The main thing in life is to avoid trouble, because troubles will find you anyway. Therefore, it makes no sense to attract trouble unnecessarily. Trouble is easy to get into and hard to get out of. It is best to stay out of trouble.

Mind Your Thoughts

Stay calm and do not let insane thoughts come in your mind, and if they come which sometimes they will, show them the door and stay calm.

Accessories

Accessories are not a part of us (who we are); they are apart from us always.

Mind Your Business

Another person's business is not yours, so why mind another person's business? Take care of your own business, and handle it right by perfecting the art of minding your own business.

The Gain of Nothing

Nothing excites modern man more than the prospect of material riches: silver and gold, oil, lean hogs and all the commodities, markets. For the most part, man has gained it all and remains extremely excited about future gains. The one thing that he has missed is his oneness with all; without it he has gained nothing at all.

Use Wisdom

Use wisdom in all things, which is what it is for, to use. Without it we become worse off than a fool.

The Acts That Dent

Life is like driving: you must know the rules and follow the signs. When it says "dead end," it is true. When it says "one way only," it means it. Now, you can go against the rules; however, it may cost you or someone else their life. Just as in driving you have to consider the others; you are not the only one on the road of life. On the evening news I saw a fatal accident caused by someone who tried to pass in a no-passing zone. The driver who caused the accident thought he could make it. An accident is caused by our acts that cause a dent in our lives or the lives of others. When we see the crushed vehicles, there are crushed lives also. Life is a road we are all on simultaneously. We must drive with care and avoid acts that dent.

Watch Your Mouth!

As for our mouth there are only two things to watch. What goes in it and what comes out of it. Now, watch your mouth!

Seek and Find in Time

There are times when finding where something is not is as important as finding where something is.

Rejoice

Rejoice whenever you can! Love whenever you can! Laugh whenever you can! Give the best of yourself whenever you can!

Too Bad

We love our illusions; it is too bad they are not real. We love our cars, money, homes, shoes, and a thousand other things; it's too bad our illusions do not love us back. God is real and we should really love God, who really loves us.

Judge Judy?

I have decided to be only an observer in life. What sense does it make to go around judging people? It takes time in my mind to arrange the court, put on my robe, get my gavel ready. Not only am I the judge, I am also the jury and the executioner! Judge Judy is paid millions of dollars a year to do what I have been doing for free. Have I lost my mind? No. I quit executing judgment on people. Judge Judy can handle it.

One with God

There is power in being one with God.

Remember Forgiveness

Perhaps we must remember to forget, as well as forget to remember.

P.O.V.

There are as many points of view as there are points to view from. If we were to see everything from love's point of view, instead of lust, perversion and other forms of error, we would love the view that points to love. Learn to accept everyone's point of view as their point of view. It does not mean that you agree, nor does it mean they are right. Every point will have two opposing points. Draw an arrow and see for yourself.

New Understanding

The understanding must come first, and then what is understood can be applied correctly.

Time Bomb

Living inside a human body is like living inside a time bomb: you never know when it's going to go off. Until it goes off!

A Crippling Thought

A crippled mind infested with crippling thoughts is worse than having a crippled body and a well mind.

Improvement

To improve anything, starting small is better than nothing at all.

Being Here Now

When you think, *Where will I be ten years from now?* you are there, only you may not have articulated it on a conscious level. Your thoughts brought you there.

What Makes the Difference?

It is amazing how a little difference can make a big difference.

No Negatives, Please

You don't need to add the negative to something that you want to turn out positive; it only works against that which you desire

Incorrectly Said

Politically incorrect, grammatically incorrect, socially incorrect, and financially incorrect. You say I am saying it wrong, I don't mind saying it wrong as long as you hear it. Right?

Time Takes Things

I know that things take time and that time takes things.

So Glad

I am so glad that I don't define my self-worth by the automobile I drive, the home I own, jewelry or money, for if I did, I would be worth nothing at all.

The Serenity Prayer

If we do not master the serenity prayer, we will not have serenity.

Pleasure/Pain

In this life we are either seeking its pleasures or searching for a way out of its pain, yet neither is anything more than a memory. And a memory is actually neither.

Lasting Beauty

Staying beautiful on the inside will keep you beautiful on the outside. However, staying beautiful on the outside does little for keeping you beautiful on the inside.

Sharing the Earth

We share the earth with all creatures, a few of which are deadly, and too many to which we are deadly.

Having Is Nothing

Whenever we equate who we are with what we have or have not, we have nothing.

~ *Wisdom's Poetry* ~

Wisdom is the deal when you keep it real; it becomes the only antidote, for a fool and his money soon departs. When you're young you want to brag and wag that tongue, but as you get older you learn to keep it in your holster.

Shooting off at the mouth gets a fool in trouble, and if they can't shut up, that trouble will double. A few wise words will speak the truth, but a fool's overflow will attract a rebuke.

Chapter 5

~ LOVE ~

One evening I decided to ask a friend a question about love. "If I poured you a glass of love, would you drink it?" The text came back, "Every drop." I replied, "Then your heart is ready for love, what an amazing answer." What is the greatest power that created the universe, that formed the earth and its inhabitants? Love. What is our greatest longing, our first need upon birth and our greatest memory in old age? Love. In this thought of love we are introduced to all that there is or ever will be. We are made of love, yet we think we can make love when it is love that makes love. If we examine the ills of our world, the wars, diseases, injustices, infidelities, poverty, famines, droughts, natural disasters, genocides, political corruption, crimes, sex slavery, greed, and hatred, to name a few, you might wonder what love is there that the world is created from. Love is the primary source of creation, the source is God, and God is love.

So what happened? How can this be love? We have distorted love just as if we took a cucumber and placed it in a blender it would become so distorted that we couldn't identify it as a complete cucumber anymore. But the truth is that it's still a cucumber in every way. If the distortion could be undone the cucumber would appear in all its glory. God the ancient eternal being has never been distorted. But our minds, with our thoughts and feelings have been distorted to the point that we have a distorted perception of love. But all is not lost, for "love," which is God source, never fails to undo distortion and bring the cucumber back into form. Hence, all is love, has been and will always be love. So if you're ready, welcome back to love undistorted.

* * So Much * *

There is so much love.

Show and Tell

"Have I told you lately that I love you?" needs to be upgraded to "Have I shown you lately that I love you?" We know that our actions speak louder than our inaction, and our actions often speak louder than words.

Seven Billion to Love

Let's see how many people you love today by starting with the person in the mirror.

If You Want to Be

If you want to be a writer, start writing, If you want to be a singer, start singing. If you want to be an painter, start painting, If you want to be a friend, be friendly. If you want to be a lover, start loving.

You Are You

You are everything God loves!

Love Is Wrong

Whenever our definition of love is wrong, love can never be right. However, when the definition of love is right, love can never be wrong.

True Judgment

I only judge you worthy of love.

Don't You Know How Much I Love You?

You can love me only with as much love as you have for yourself. You cannot give me a dollar if you have only a dime for yourself.

Give It

In many relationships, we are secretly interested in what we can get from the relationship, instead of what we can give. If our focus is on giving, then we will naturally receive, because receiving is a natural by-product of giving, and not the other way around.

Children's View of Love

The best thing for a father to show his children is to love their mother, and the best thing for a mother to show her children is to love their father. The children love them both; they need to know that love and respect form the nucleus of the family unit, thereby knowing that they are a family of love.

Very Little

Trying to make people righteous when you are not righteous is a shame/sham! There is very little you can do with people that will make them anything, so you might as well love them, accept them, and forgive them as they are.

There Is Room

The world is confused and exists in a state of unawareness, yet in confusion there's room for understanding, in hatred there's room for love, in war there is so much room for peace, in disease there is room for healing, in rejection there's room for acceptance, in separation there's room for unity, and in darkness there is an enormous room for light. All is contained in love.

I Look, Eye See!

Look without the I of judgment, and you will see though the eye of love. If you could see the heart of me, you would not say or do the things that hurt or limit me; you would see me through the I of love.

Love without Competition

What we send out returns to us, for what we sow we also reap; we cannot escape or fear it; we need only understand it and better our lives. When you hate those who hate you, both of you lose. When you love those who hate you, you win. Love wins in the end … every time … easily … guaranteed, yet it is not a competition at all; love simply is the winner.

Kill War with Peace

I listen to my coworkers on the job; if there is an upset or grievance, some seeming injustice by management, someone will say, "Give them hell!" In my thinking, they already have hell going on, so if you add hell to hell, will you get heaven (peace)? You get more hell. If there is a fire, do you say, "Give it more fire!"? No, you use its opposite: water. So whenever dealing with a problem, no matter its size, use love and forgiveness. When nations want peace, their solution is war, when you spell it backward, you get raw. War is as raw as we get with one another; we agree to kill one another. War cannot bring peace; only love and forgiveness can.

God's True Love

When it comes to love we must learn to love in God's way or we don't love, though we think we do. And the old saying "You always hurt the one you love" too often comes true.

The Power Of

"I love."

Just Keep Loving

I cannot love me and hate you. I cannot hate me and love you. When I love me, I love you, and when I hate you, I hate me. Just love and keep on loving.

You Deserve

If wanting something were enough to get it, then we would all have what we ever wanted. Trying is not always enough; if it were, then all of our efforts would have delivered the goods. Perhaps we must know that we deserve whatever it is before we can have it. If we carry guilt in our lives, we cannot really feel deserving of anything.

Love Thought

All it takes is for the two of us to resonate on the same frequency of love; nothing else matters. This is a truer meaning of what being in love is, the truest meaning is being together in God; harmony is oneness resonating love. Love is the greatest of all, for it loves all, love is you and we are one in love. Love is always giving and receiving. Love is all there is.

The Love Rise

When I think of love, and how misused, misconstrued, and abused it is, a word so often inappropriately used, perhaps that's why we are feeling screwed and blue after falling for the words "I love you." Doubt enters the picture; trust exits the door of our hearts. Who of us can live without love? Our definition of love is flawed, our expectations so grand, and its promises so fleeting, leaving all without it so needing. Can a substitute satisfy or pacify one's heart? Lust is but an impostor, a lie masquerading as the truth, leaving us empty and vulnerable to the dis-ease of a broken heart. Perhaps love is not what we think or feel it is. First we are in love, and then we are not in love. What madness, what folly! True love is flawless in expression and eternal. As we align our hearts with love, we will no longer fall in love, we shall rise in love, become one in love. Come rise with me, my love; regrets will be no more.

Light/Love

Light illuminates, bringing enlightenment. It always gives of itself; never does it take from another. Light and love are one and the same. This reminds me of the candle that lights another. It loses nothing by giving its all.

In All Ways

I will love you always and forever, and in all ways will you be loved.

* * *Love Power* * *

People who love power often step on those with none; however, those with love power lift those with none.

The Body of Love

When all fear has been purged from the body, you become the embodiment of love.

Inner Peace

It's okay now … I can love.

Are You Plugged In?

There is so much I feel being plugged into love, for that is what I am.

Judgeless Instead of Loveless

I try to be judgeless, not loveless. When I judge less, I will not love less. Less judgment means more love meant. The more I love you, the less I judge you. All who judge are also judged, while all who observe are only observed not judging. It is best to use love meant instead of judgment. Too often we look at others with our judgment; however, we should love others as love meant.

Human Armor

Fear and vulnerability, uncertainty and suspicion call for protective armor. We cannot see the defensive person inside; we know they are hiding, afraid of being attacked. What if they knew they were only to be loved? We all could live without the weighty armor and be free as love intended and begin to levitate and meditate on the higher expressions of life.

Another

To beat another is to beat one; to help another is to help one. To love another is to love one another.

Earth Dove

Of all the creatures on earth, you are a dove, my love.

Impossible to Love

One cannot love corruption, injustice, or evil, for they are incompatible with love.

Lust and Love

Love is forgiving. Lust is for taking. Our minds seem to be set on auto-lust instead of auto-love; our minds seem to be set on auto-judge, auto-jury, and auto-executioner, instead of love, non-judgment, and forgiveness. What if we consciously reset our minds to love? Would it reset our lives?

Time to Love

This is the time to love: while we have breath, while we have feeling, while we have time, while we have expression, while we have each other. This is the time to love.

Owe No One

Owe no one anything but to love them. When we love, we seldom judge; when we judge, we seldom love.

The Greatest Opportunity

I cannot pass up the opportunity to love you each day in every way, down to the last detail. It's all or not love at all, yet it must start with you.

Love Flow

Let love flow. That is what it's made for.

Oneness

There is only one air, one water, one earth, one people, and one love.

Love Fact

I got it! It's all about love. If we do not love, we have nothing! I mean, dead-broke nothing!

Love Peace

Love brings much peace.

Peace of Love

A piece of this and a piece of that, but the peace of love is whole.

The Love Carrier

Love will carry you as you carry it. Become a carrier of love, and be carried by love.

Nothing But Cool

By loving one, I love all, for we are all one. It is not possible to love any other way. Love is whole, not fragmented. It is the way we choose to love that is fragmented or in part. One must be whole to love wholly; if one is fragmented so is one's expression of love. The definition of cool is having a heart that is open to love. It's just that simple.

Love Flow

Love flows like water; it hydrates your soul. Drink all you want; it makes your heart happy and whole. All that's needed is a willing soul for love to flow.

The Touch

The wind touches us all, the water touches us all, the earth touches us all, and love touches us all. It's time for us to touch the wind with love, touch the water with love, touch the earth with love, and touch one another with love.

Changing

I no longer pray that you will change; instead I pray that I will change, so that I can love you unconditionally. You see, it's about me changing, and that is it. When I change, everything changes; when I do not change, everything stays the same.

Love, Why Try? ... Become

There comes a time in a person's life when they try to give love. Then there comes a time when they try to get love. And if they are lucky, there comes a time when they just become love. Now they're cooking.

Love Life, of Course!

How is your love life? "I love life." No, how is your love life? "It's on course." What I mean is how is it? "I love life of course."

Love's Riches

I have deep pockets of love. My heart flying in love beats stronger every day. In fifty thousand years I will still be loving you.

Ruin

Some people ruin their financial life because they know nothing about money; some ruin their health because they know nothing about their bodies' needs. Some people ruin their minds, morals, ethics, dignity, and reputations because they lack the knowledge of love for themselves.

Romantic Thought

To what lengths will a man go to see the woman he loves? To such lengths I have gone for you.

Love Exists

The true love that you thought does not exist … exists! I am that love. Moreover, the love I knew always existed exists as you.

Love, Not Fear

Where there is love, there can be no fear; and where there is fear, there will be no love.

I'll Take Your Hate

Everything is love, your hate is love distorted. I'll take your hate, transmute it by love's alchemy back into its perfect state, send it back to you as a double blessing. I'll take your hate and send you love. Thank you.

* * *Everybody Has to Learn Sometime* * *

Why try to change anyone? They are who they are, or they aren't who they are. I accept who they are and who they aren't. Everybody has to learn unconditional love sometime. If you can't love who they are, love who they aren't; and if you can't love who they aren't, then love who they are.

* * *Being Love* * *

I open to my eternal state of being ... love.

* * *I Have Love* * *

I have found love. It was with me all along. I can love again, rejoice and celebrate.

Loving Love

I love, love, love I love.

My Love

That you may be affected by my love.

Don't You Know

That "I love you" is not a temporary thing?

How 'Bout That Sound?

God says to love and treat you right. I am willing, and there is nothing that you can do about it.

Love Never Stops

Falling in love is great; it is the stopping that hurts so badly. Solution: never stop loving. Keep on loving, for in truth love never stops.

Reject, Accept, Love!

If they reject you, they reject me. If they accept you, they accept me. When they love you, they love me. When they see you, they see me.

Secret Fears

When we release our secret fears, love will no longer seem like a secret kept from us.

Television

My dearest love, last night I dreamed of you, and now you are here. I promise my undying love. I heard it on tell a vision.

Black Pepper

One day the pepper shaker fell six feet onto my foot. I responded by repeating the word *love*. The pain diminished quickly. This is what love does to our pain: it diminishes it quickly. This painful experience encouraged me to broaden my expectations of love, gain a greater understanding of love, and use the power and potential of love at all times and in all ways. Love is here to help us in a multitude of diverse ways. The door has opened; will you enter the world of love without pain?

Heart Strings

As I strum the strings of my heart, may the sound thereof go out to you.

Show and Tell

My simply telling you that I love you would not be enough, but my showing you that I love you would be enough, so that my simply telling you would be enough, because I backed it up by showing you that I love you.

Fear War, Love Peace

Fear drives war, while love drives peace! Fear attacks, while love holds back attack.

Up to Us

Everything negative that exists is because we give it expression. If we expressed only love, the ills of the world could exist no more.

Create a World of Love

I am creating a world of love. You are invited; you may come and go as you please, but this is where I Am. Therefore, love is all that my consciousness creates in the I Am world of love. Welcome.

Who?

Who can sing the song of the heart, and who can hear the song except the one who sings the same song?

I Am

I am loved, admired, valued, and desired.

One Thought

Love: one size fits all!

The Light Is Love

Light is impartial; it shines on all. Love is impartial, for it loves all. If plants receive no light, they do not grow. If we receive no light, there is no growth either. The more light, the more growth. The more love means more love for all. I speak of the Christ who is the love light or the light of love, the same that came to help us grow.

If

If you love, you need do nothing else. If you love not, you are doing everything that does not need doing.

Love World

When people come into my world of love, they find nothing but love.

Suspended Forever

I have suspended judgment, criticism, and ridicule henceforth, now and forever, as my heart and mind are open for love and the endless possibilities thereof.

We Cannot, We Must

Sit down and think about life. We cannot treat others any old way and expect to not reap what we have sown. We must try to help one another and do what is good while we have life. We must love while we have time. We must be kind while we have time. We must hear while we can, and talk to one another while we have voice. We must open our eyes as well as our hearts and feel while we can. We must sit down and think about life; we cannot afford not to.

Start Loving

Love is a start you never stop; we must start with love, or we will end without it.

Too Late!

You can be late for dinner, and you can be late for work; you can be late for an appointment, or late for your first child's birth. However, it's never too late to love.

Race and Culture

The illusion tricks us into believing we should hate because of our differences, yet in reality we should love everyone the same.

To Be Loved

To feel unloved is like drowning one's spirit. To be loved brightens the darkest night, brings health to the body, and cheers up the heart. All we need is to be loved.

Weightlifting

Just a show of love can lift the heavy weights we carry.

Emptiness

I see into the empty soul, I feel its emptiness; I can fill that emptiness with tears of love, understanding, compassion, and kindness, tears that can wash away the fears that haunt the empty soul.

Being Inseparable

It is wonderful that love and peace are inseparable. Remember this always, my love, and we two shall never part.

The Moment

We are told to live in the moment, instead of the past or the future. They tell us to capture the moment. How do you capture the moment, and by what means? Is life not lived one moment at a time? With a camera, we can capture the moment. Then we are living in the next moment. This is my answer. It came to me today. Living in the moment means accepting unconditional love and unconditional forgiveness as my only reality.

One at a Time

We can say only one word at a time, take one step at a time, breathe one breath at a time, eat one meal at a time, and live one day at a time, yet we can love all, all of the time.

Grown Children

We are all just grown children still in need of love.

The Love

Love can always deal with a situation better than hatred, and forgiveness can deal better with a situation than un-forgiveness.

Love Deficiency

When people are unreasonable, they need more love. When people blow themselves up, they need more love. Whenever you see the ills of others acted out on others, there is a reason, and we all need more love. Love is God functioning in the heart.

The Origin of Dysfunction

Without oneness people tend to destroy themselves; without oneness they become quickly dysfunctional. By dysfunctional, I mean they live a life outside of oneness with love, which creates a multitude of problems. Humanity's only function is to function as one with love. Apart from this is the dysfunction we see, whether it be in children or adults.

The Prostitute Thought

The prostitute may think her family has withdrawn from her, society loathes her, police seek to arrest her, men abuse her, and, surely, no one loves her. She thinks she is a worthless prostitute who has lost her dignity. Nevertheless, God loves her and understands and will restore her dignity, for she shall access the kingdom of heaven before many, and she shall be free of shame, she shall be whole, she shall be loved as God's beloved. She is my daughter, my sister, my spouse, my friend. Love is all she ever was.

Know No

Know that I love you and me; can there be any other way? No.

Like

Like a peacock loves his feathers, like a dog loves wagging his tail, like a snail loves his shell, like a star loves to shine, like I love to love you all the time.

Sacred Love Vow

I pray that I will bring much joy, laughter, happiness, and comfort to you. In addition, I pray that you will bring much joy, laughter, happiness, and comfort to me. That our vow will be eternally kept by the perfect love of God, maintained by our inner Christ self, and fueled by the Holy Spirit, which keeps us whole in every way. That our home be sacred, always tended with tenderness, continuous in oneness, desiring each other always. Knowing and experiencing the special bond we share I stand fast with you in love, my beloved.

Thoughts on the Vow

The sacred love vow entered my thought on July 26, 2003. It is based on perfect love, a love that is whole, and a love that is supported by a higher power. This vow is 100 percent positive; there is no sickness, no poverty, no bad times, and no separation by death. It covers the whole person. It is an advanced thought, a vow with new expectation and promise. What the traditional vow does is keep tradition going; if you included the sickness and health, for good or for bad, for poverty or wealth, and in death do we part, you have a 50/50 admixture of thought expectation. You opened the door in your mind for sickness, poverty, separation, and death, all of which are the enemy of your vow. Tradition is strong, and it often rules us, but truth is stronger than tradition. Will you choose truth or tradition?

Feeling Wonderful

What is wonderful about loving someone? It's that they cause you to feel; you feel inspired to love and be loved, which is a wonderful feeling.

A Love Pursuit

A man cannot pursue a love that does not exist, but he can have a love that does.

To Love Is Everything

Having nothing is really something, and having something is really nothing, but to love is everything.

Keep Peeling Away

Since love is the essence, the core and source of who we truly are, we must start to peel away the layers of fear that have encapsulated and prevented us in this life from knowing the true source of our being. Like the peeling of the onion, which causes our tears, as we keep peeling we will learn to live without fear.

Why We Love Children

A thought about why we love children. Like Christ the children have not yet forgotten how to live and how to love. I think we are fascinated with their capacity for unconditional love and forgiveness, something most adults have long not seen or felt in their hearts. Children know only play, fun, and laughter; they are not at all serious about life and never would they create weapons and reason for war. Perhaps they make us feel what we thought we were incapable of feeling again. Unless we become as a little child, we cannot enter the kingdom of heaven within.

Giving Up

When a man gives up on love, he turns to lust and loses his greatness. When a man gives up on lust, he turns to love and finds his greatness.

Life without Love

A life without love is like a tree without leaves, like a mountain without a top, like an ocean without water.

In Love Alone

No one wants to be in love alone. Too often we end up in lust together with another, and in love alone. Being alone is not to be feared; it is to be understood.

My Wonderful You

There is something wonderful about you that I love; it is you.

Heart's Desire Thought

Having you makes me roar like a lion, soar like an eagle, shine like the sun, and move like the wind.

My

My thoughts are very deep, my insides crystal clear, my eyes pierce the soul, my mouth speaks the truth, my heart beats for you, my ears hear the bird sing, my touch is ever gentle, my fragrance I inhale, my life I give to you, my love is ever true.

Cool Love

Loving is cool, and that is being cool enough!

A Friend's Good-bye

Never like to see you go, will be glad to have you back, and I hope to see you sooner than later.

Heart to Heart

When we talk heart to heart, it is ear to ear, in which we hear to hear, with the art to art of the heart to heart, which travels from heart to ear in which we hear the art of the heart when we talk heart to heart.

Say Nothing, Say Everything

You touched my soul by saying nothing, which says everything.

Love Chant

If we all agreed to do a love chant together, focused as one, we could surely change the course of history in the making for the betterment of us all. We could energize the air, the ether, the atmosphere, and eliminate fear; we could brighten the sky, enrich the earth, open the minds and hearts of millions. The melodic sounds we would sing to celebrate and praise love would inspire us, support us, prosper us, and love us, in the love chant.

Deathless Love

I only ask for your undying, everlasting love for me, and in return, I promise an immortal, endless, and eternal love for you.

A Healing Love

I am sending a healing love to you; it will be there, and it will heal you and love you no later than now.

This Is the Time!

This is the time to love, while we have breath, while we have feeling, while we have time, while we have expression; this is the time to forgive while we can give, this is the time to love!

Living without Love

When we attempt to live without love in our lives, it twists our perceptions. So great is the need for love that without it we are like a person at the North Pole with only a pair of jeans and a T-shirt. So great is the need that perception is altered, where the desire to cuddle with a polar bear may seem logical, rather than freeze without the warmth of love.

Love

Love is a wonderful thing to have. The more one has, the more one gives.

The more one gives, the more one receives, the more one receives, the more one gives. Love is a wonderful thing to have to give.

The Attitudes and Moods

If a person has eight hundred attitudes and four hundred moods, skip it; you can do better with someone who has the right attitude and is in the mood for love.

New Love-based Thought

I came, I saw, I cared, I loved, and I made a positive difference in the lives of many people. Love conquers by coming, seeing, and caring enough to love, thereby making a positive difference in the lives of many people.

Love Never Fails

Seeing that we were created in love by love, filled inside and covered outside with love, why do you suppose we fail at love?

Love Understanding People

It's all about how you see people. If you see them as something to take advantage of, you will try to take advantage of them. If you see them as unworthy, then you will treat them as unworthy. But if you see them through the eyes of love and understanding, you will understand and love them, for this is what the people need, love and understanding.

Make It Big Love

In our modern world, we want to make it big in life; we want bigger homes, bigger cars, bigger yachts, and big money! Some women want bigger breasts, and some men want a bigger penis. In all this frenzy about bigger being better, has anyone considered the desire for a bigger heart, one that includes rather than excludes, a heart enlarged with love?

Love Today

We are here today, and therefore we should love today, for tomorrow will come but is not promised.

Things Can't Love

Isn't it funny that the things we love can't love us back? Not the car, the home, our clothes, jewelry, pizza, sports, vacation homes, money, or our favorite movies and TV shows. Not even our most loved and cherished songs. Yet we love these things unconditionally. Isn't it funny how we find unconditional love for things and not one another?

Earning Respect

To be a man or woman is to earn the respect of others, not by force or fear, but by the way you handle yourself and others in real-life situations with respect and love.

Love Art

The art of the heart is love!

What Comes from the Heart Reaches the Heart

An open heart forgives and gives for the sake of giving. An open heart is a big heart that has space for friend and stranger alike, accepts humanity as family. It says, *I have a space in my heart for you.* An open heart is able to expand; it is flexible, strong, and healthy. It has wisdom and love, can see those in need, gives unconditionally of itself. It is a willing heart, a heart that trusts; a heart that grows is a heart that glows. Its value is priceless. It is a smiling heart that beats freely. Those who develop such a heart possess a heart that beats with the great eternal heart of God.

A Closed Heart

There are closed hearts that are small and petty, which have only enough space for themselves. The closed heart lets nothing in and gives nothing out. It is hard as stone, weak and unhealthy, fearful and foolish. It harbors hatred and judgments, resentment and negativity. It sees only its own needs and dismisses the needs of others. It is an unwilling heart that is dull and sluggish. It kills joy for its own miserable state.

Are We Open or Closed?

This is the time to open our hearts, to nourish and encourage, to feel the love the warmth and the magic. The purpose and desire of our heart is to open with love and forgiveness. If you ask, "Why forgive?" Just as life is for living, you will also find that love is forgiving. We live in a world of offenses; forgiveness is essential for our survival. Superiority is not race, color, creed, or national origin; instead we find it in those who live with open hearts. A person with a closed heart is like a business with a "closed" sign in the window; you cannot come in, communicate, or do business. An open heart says, "Come in. We're open." An open heart is ready to receive, while the closed heart does not know how receive. Most hearts fall somewhere in between.

Side Effects

Of all the medicine that man has made to cure ill with an elixir or a pill, we do find still another potential ill from his elixir and his pill. The side effects are sometimes worse than the illness, causing blindness, stroke, suicidal thoughts and actions, heart attack, and even sudden death. God's prescription for our ills is love; it may sound too easy, does not cost a cent, and, best of all, works without any side effects. So if you feel you must take a chance with medicine, make sure you take a daily dose of love, as much as you can take, and share it with everyone that you meet.

Heir to Love

Love is like the air; it is everywhere, everyone needs it all the time, and without it we become dysfunctional. Did you know that you are an heir to love?

Love All Today

I send out love to all, for all need love today.

That's Right

I am sending you love and light and all that's right.

Keep On Loving

One thing is certain: a writer must keep on writing, a painter must keep on painting, and a lover must keep on loving.

Love Everybody

Too often we stop at loving just one person. We have to love everybody. It is extremely important that people know that they are loved. If they have a body, you have to love everybody.

Love Sound

There is the love of sound, and there is the sound of love. Love is sound!

The Love Song

You are the love song my heart loves to sing.

The Power Walk

You can walk in love's power only when the power of love walks in you.

~ *Love's Poetry* ~

It was a brisk day as I looked upon the strawberry fields. I imagined all that could be true if I only believed. Suddenly I was taken to a meadowland full of wild grasses, as I glanced toward the horizon, the sea-pink sky was mingled with a French blue hue. This I knew was me and you in the world we could share if we only believed. I noticed a golden flicker, which blinded me for a moment, and then the voice of an angel spoke softly in my ear, "Follow the ocean blue until you discover the mystic pool on the Isle of Capri," and with the sound of a distant thunder sped away at the speed of wonderful light. I followed a pathway that only I had trod. I could see the footprints of a fragile beauty a perfect part of me, yes she would be. It was a timeless day as I strolled on in a peaceful way, and as the evening approached so did I follow a sparkling silver spring decorated so lovely with the scent of Siberian iris and delicate tones fresh in the air of gardenia punctuated every inhalation of life I drew easily into my nostrils. I came to a tropical forest rich in wild bamboo; tree ferns and jungle moss I used to create a tree house for me and for you. For all that I am is all that you are, and what I do for me, I do for you, my sweet china doll; and in the morning I will go up hills and down golden valleys in search of English cucumbers so fresh with sun dew. I picture eating them with thrilled delight with you. Like an elusive fawn in the forest of my heart, I will find the jewel of heaven as an exotic blossom; you are fragrant and potent as rare wine, and the summer melon is not to be compared to the sweetness of our peach tree love. You are a water lily lotus in the formal sunken garden of my heart: my sugar plum, delicate bloom, first blush; there I saw you as the filtered sun shown through the violet veil, violet dimensions reveal your golden peach tree smile shining as the desert sunrise in all its crowning glories. It would be an elegant evening, starlight would fill our mood with a Swiss blue sky and a magnificent valley view, our feet together in the warm dewy grasses we step with the lightness of an angel's wing, eyes fixed in the candle glow of love, the cool pink ice that enhances the more as we drink the nectar of love like richness of butter cream from the tulips of good we both in a timeless way "make love" our silver lagoon habitation of eternal serenity. As Vienna Lake reflected the island sunset we relaxed into the evening in love.

Chapter 6

~ SPIRIT ~

The spirit is that intangible part of us that directly connects us to the source, the father/mother of all spirits. It is that which quickens, giving us animation in the physical realm. It is not limited to our five senses; neither is it limited to the physical body. It is deathless, ageless, formless, substance of light. It is the talking light, the smallest particle, and the size of the universe and beyond; it is the God self. It is what you really are.

* * The Empty Filling * *

The emptiness will be more than what they can fill. But I shall feel their emptiness and fill their emptiness.

Spiritual Unfolding

Unfolding in the physical realm reaches its prime around thirty years of age and moves toward folding up. Spiritual unfolding never stops or folds up, and that's the joy of the journey.

Within

Enlightenment comes from within. From within comes enlightenment.

Meditate Shun

In order for one to enter into deep meditation, one must understand the necessity to shun all distraction; therein lies the secret to meditate shun.

Continuous Living

Today is the sixteenth of November. I call it my birthday, which is a type of impossibility, yet we make it so. To all other life forms it is just the continuous discontinuous life, without days, dates, months, or years, the eternal now of just being.

The Christ

It was not enough for Jesus to have had understanding; it's now our time to understand that "Do unto others as you would have done unto you" means we all are one. A spiritual reality that when understood collapses the illusion of separation.

Integration

Meeting yourself for the integration of the many you's into the one to enjoy.

You Really Are

What really is, is what you really are: love, light, eternal energy, spirit, an extension of God source.

To Be

I am greater than I appear to be, and I appear to be a great spirit!

* * One Bottom Line * *

I am one with the One.

Flying Doubtless

I can fly so high, I can dance my spirit in the sky. I would show you, but you do not believe me. The gravity of your consciousness keeps you grounded. Your doubts are weighty as matter. Your fear blocks the way. Success is found when we carry these burdens no more. Watch me do it; I can fly so high, I can dance my spirit in the sky.

Super Human Spirit

Have you ever thought about what Superman, Batman, and Wonder Woman actually represent? Superman is about willingness to help those less fortunate; the kryptonite represents negative forces or thoughts that diminish his power. Batman and Robin go to bat in the defense of Gotham City; while Wonder Woman shows her virtues with a golden lasso, making would-be liars tell the truth. These heroes have great strength of mind; their thoughts are extraordinary. Never giving up the fight for justice, they leave an imprint on our minds that we too have the potential for betterment. That is what makes you a super human spirit.

It's Unreal

Illusionary people with illusionary minds thinking illusionary thoughts live illusionary lives in an illusionary world, and that is no illusion.

Mind Time

One person on the job thinks the week is going slow, another person does not think so, and another thinks it is going fast. The week is going neither fast nor slow; it is all in the mind time.

A Great Secret

I have learned a great secret today that is no longer a secret to me. However, it remains great. It has to do with returning to oneness. Separate yourself only from the thought/belief of separation only. Oneness will be the result.

Are You the Judge?

It is good in life to be an observer who needs not judge what is observed. There is no need for jury duty, no executioner's rope. Just observe and remember to observe your thoughts. Be aware of it all. remember it is just from your perspective.The most important thing to do when observing others is to observe yourself.

Free New Life

To be free of lack and attachment would be a free new life.

I See

As I see you, I must see me; as I see me, I must see you.

Find Thought

I could not find what was not there.

You Know You

What matters is that you know you are not what people think you are.

Have Fun!

Appearances are just fun for us to play with, not to take seriously or make real.

Free, Go in Peace

Free yourself from the expectations of others, free others from expectations, and go in peace.

Life Is But a Dream

If you were to awaken within a dream, what would you do? Where would you go? What would you become? In a dream you can do things like fly. When awake what can you do in a dream?

Getting Closer

The closeness gets only closer until we realize again our oneness with the one and one another. You need to understand what getting closer entails. When you go to sleep, you are getting closer to waking up, and the moment you awaken, you are getting closer by the second to sleep once again. The further away you get from one, the closer you get to the other.

I Am Here Today

I am greater today than yesterday, because I am still here today.

You Army

When you see yourself as one with everyone, how could you want anyone? When you no longer want, you will have freedom from wanting the way you do now. When you see yourself as one with everyone, you will find no reason to attack anyone again. When you see that you are me, and there is only one race; the human race, you will begin to understand the you army.

Spiritual Mirrors

Before there were any human-made mirrors, there was the still water in which one could see one's own reflection and contemplate who they saw as them. Water being a symbol of spirit translates into this understanding. One cannot truly know oneself unless one looks to spirit to reflect back one's true spiritual identity.

Mini-Max

Minimum effort that brings about maximum results is a great thought that needs manifestation, for we often find ourselves in the opposite arrangement, which is putting forth maximum effort that brings about minimal results. This I believe to be a major divine design principle. When you plant an apple seed, you do so with minimal effort that yields maximum results, thousands upon thousands of apples for however long apple trees yield apples.

Greatness!

I still have the great power of Spirit.

Spiritual

There are two kinds of human beings living on earth; one is evolved, and the other is UN-evolved. What I find fascinating is how so many of us have evolved from being hunter-gatherers, to the industrial revolution, to our present technology, yet there remain remnants of people who live in remote jungles who do not know what a cell phone is. These are the UN-evolved. Yet spiritually this ratio is reversed; most human beings are spiritually UN- evolved, still living in the dark jungle of their lower consciousness, while there is a remnant of highly evolved spiritual people in their midst. These shall be the lights of the world; they shall help the UN-evolved come up higher.

Holy Consciousness

Consciousness must be part of the whole. To not know the whole is to operate in partial consciousness. If we are not fully conscious, then we are half awake and half asleep. In such a state nothing can be fully understood. This is the state of humanity. Perhaps diseases like cancer are conscious matter operating out from the wholeness wreaking havoc and bringing death. The Christ would say, Be made whole! (Not separated.)

Identity

I am the joyful one!

Serious Life Thought

Have you heard someone say they are going to get something out of this life? Well that is the point: to get life out of life. You are not here to die but to live, and not die.

Higher-Frequency Thoughts

Everything we see has been the expression of the mortal mind of humanity. The immortal has yet to be expressed, seen, or experienced.

The New Image

Doing away with the mortal image that has been held firmly in the mind, a new, immortal image is emerging and is now here! It may sound strange, but if three hundred years ago someone had said, "I see humans eating and drinking in the sky above the clouds, moving at enormous speeds," they would have been called a lunatic. Can you imagine if they'd said they saw men on the moon?

The Power Lies Dormant

There has been more belief in what is outside of us than in what lies dormant within us, and we suffer needlessly.

Trust Me

I will not let you down. I will lift you up until you can view the greatness of yourself for yourself. I can see it for you, but I want you to see it; then it will have been worth it. Trust me.

Talent

You must claim your talent, for only then can it prosper in your hand.

The New Walk

One day while walking down a road in Mississippi, I asked God, *Teach me how to walk, show me the way.* The following was downloaded into my consciousness: *Our parents teach us to walk like them, and we learn. I will teach you to walk in peace, in love, in wholeness.*

The Christ Expansion Thought

When there is enough light, there is no darkness. When there is enough life, there is no death. When there is enough love, there is no hatred. When there is enough health, there is no illness. When there is enough Christ consciousness manifested in humanity, darkness, death, hatred, and illness will no longer exist.

Free the Slave

My place in the world is not to be a slave working for others; my place in this world is to free those who are slaves to the world's illusion.

Pure Divinity Thought

My thoughts have become increasingly pure. I am so thankful to be delivered from the corruption of the mind to that which is divine.

Unlimited Powerful Thought

I am turning this over to my God self.

Prayerfully True

We will continue to pray, "God do this and that," as long as we believe that we are separated from God. What if God worked through you to do this and that? You would experience the same oneness that Jesus did.

See Nothing But the Light

I observe everything and every thought in the light, and I fear no thing. When you hold it before the light, the light will show you what cannot be seen in the dark. The light will instruct you to do this; the light will present the question, "Tell me, what do you see?" If you answer, "I see only the light," the light will gently smile at you. If you see anything other than the light, you have not seen the light; you are not ready.

The Burden

The burden is the flesh of the ego.

Umm Hmm!

Most people have eyes yet do not see, have ears yet cannot hear, have minds yet do not understand. I say this for I have seen, heard, and understood that which cannot be seen, heard, or understood.

Disease

The ultimate disease to overcome is death.

Special Education

We all need special education, for it consists of learning higher truths, gaining greater understanding, and exercising our spiritual faculties.

Get the Point

In all things taught or spoken by the Christ, there was always a point, and when people miss the point, they tend to go off in many unnecessary directions. His sayings were pointing the way to understanding, in knowing the truth.

Completely New Light

To say I see women in a completely new light is to see them in the light; in the light there is no lust, only love. You cannot see darkness in the light. However, you can see light in the darkness.

Centering Yourself

I have found that centering myself three times a day will collapse the unreal world, and it falls away.

Looking Within

Every day I look up at the sky and see that it all comes from within.

Deathless Will

People make out their wills; the only will I have is to live. There is no place for death unless you will make a place.

Unbelief

Someone in the Bible said "Help thou my unbelief." The unbelief is sickness and death over wholeness and life.

Inspire Me

Inspire me to touch the soul, mind, and spirit, for that is greater than touching the body.

Crooked Thoughts

The majority of humanity has what I will call crooked thoughts; these thoughts are not in alignment with the divine mind, which brings forth perfection. Our crooked thoughts wear us down, by the crooked decisions we make, the stupid things we do, and the misery and regrets that often follow. If crooked teeth can be corrected, our thoughts can be corrected also. Step one: no longer be content with crooked thoughts. Step two: ask for the divine mind to open up a new stream of thought to you. These new thoughts help straighten our crooked thinking by gently bringing our thoughts into alignment with divine mind..

I Am

I am going to reach that dimension within my being where I am no longer bound by what I see, hear, touch, taste, or smell. At such a point, I will see love, hear love, touch love, taste love, and smell love, for I Am love.

A Prayer Thought

The greatest prayer that can be prayed is by the Christ self within; such a prayer cannot go unanswered.

** * Spirit Thought * **

We are going into the Spirit now.

Genius Thought

I am a genius whose thoughts will influence the thoughts of millions.

Since God Sense

Since the only thing that makes any sense in my life right now is God, I can find no sense in the world.

The Soaring Thought

Most people can fly, but few soar. One must fly before one can soar. Flying takes a lot of effort and energy to keep from falling to the earth, but as we climb higher in consciousness, the wings of our minds are caught up by the great heavenly winds, we start to soar and relax, we see the big picture, and we are climbing higher and higher until we are seen no more.

Perceptions

We are divided only by our perceptions of one another. Our perceptions are subject to error; once our perceptions are corrected, they will no longer divide us but will express our oneness.

* * Pure Thought * *

My thoughts have become so pure, I can cause no damage. I can only increase the good in all.

* * The Need for Prayer * *

There are people who have never been prayed for, whose lives are living nightmares.

The Forgiveness Conference

If it is killing you inside, it's not worth it; the time for positive change has come. I will help you let it go.

Life Force

Life force is energy, the driving power of your being. When you allow this force to be channeled into negative emotions, it empowers the negative, which decreases your life force energy. Your life force energy can be used for the positive that you need and desire.

Go in Peace

Wherever I go, I go in peace, and whenever I leave, I leave in peace, and I leave my peace with you.

I Am Awake

You cannot tell them you are awake. How can a person in a deep sleep possibly know you are awake? Only those who are awake know those who are awake. They who are awake know they who are asleep. The sleeper never knows he was asleep until he is fully awake!

Projecting Peace

When we are at peace within, we project peace outwardly.

Projecting Your State of Mind

Whatever state of mind we are in is projected out into the world.

The World Must Be Muted

In order to hear from a higher source, one must mute the world, with all of its chatter, information, suggestions, foolishness, and insanity, and then one is ready to hear from a higher source.

The Golden Shall Rule

The golden rule states that we should do unto others as we would have others do unto us. This includes thoughts and words, not just deeds. It is the most simple concept based on mutual love and respect, but seemingly too complex for us to apply consistently. However, those who master this ancient wisdom spoken by the Christ, they shall rule in the coming age.

An Anointed Thought

What I inherited from my earthly father was darkness; what I inherited from my heavenly spiritual father is light.

Perfect Thought

I have been on a quest for the perfect thought but I don't know if the perfect thought exist.

The Salty Thought

I am the salt of the earth, the great flavor enhancer, preservative, anti-spoilage entity. All who encounter me I leave with some seasoning of love in their life. The moment they are touched by love, their life is made better; everything tastes better, smells better, feels better, sounds better, and looks better. I am the salt of the earth.

Power of Living Thought

When you can live without anxiety, you are living; when you can live without fear and doubt, you are living; when you can live without dying, you are living!

Awesome Crossing-Over Thought

There are ministers of religion, and ministers of finance, prime ministers, etc. Then there is the life minister. What is a life minister? A life minister is a religious and world deprogrammer, one who is able to administer life to another, one who has divine power to help a person cross over from death unto life, one who has the power to rebuke death and death will obey. In the present old order, a minister cannot help a person cross over from death unto life, but can only help a person cross over from life to death.

Reality Steps Forward

When you are trapped within that place in your mind, you project something into the illusion of the world that is unreal, while you remain hidden from view even from yourself. You project illusion into illusion, because that is all you know, yet you call it keeping it real when it is not. When you are no longer trapped within that place in your mind, and know the real you from the illusionary you, you will be able to project the real you in a dynamic and vibrant way. The illusion will shrink back, and reality will step forward.

You have to experience what is out there before you experience what is within, and then you will know spiritual love and fulfillment as the only reality.

The December 2006 Observation

The sky today is blue, very blue; I feel the flesh upon my face. My face has expression, many expressions of my soul. My eyes reflect like a mirror to my soul. Who can read the language of my eyes, the mirror of my soul?

Death to Death

Today I witnessed an interesting observation between two of my coworkers. One coworker said he would be forty this Saturday. The other person said, "Ah, may you live another hundred years." The man replied, "No. Maybe another forty years more; I would not want to bury my children." The other man agreed, for they both had young children. Seeing their obvious predicament, I said, "But now you have a dilemma, because children do not want to bury their parents" (the love is equal). They both looked at me as to say, *Hmm, very true.* I continued, "The only solution is to keep on living. Then one said, "Yeah! That is right!" Then I walked away. People are so programmed to die, they rarely challenge death; they simply agree with it, and they hold onto mortality like a lover. The thought of overcoming death is an alien thought, one you dare not question. Tell me who said man could not fly because he was not a bird; who said you had to die and keep on dying? I tell you, just as we started to believe and are now flying, we can start living and stop dying; in ignorance of the way, ignorance of the truth, and ignorance of the life, ignorance of Christ and the power of an endless life.

Are You Aware of Awareness?

What I witnessed today was the awareness, which judges nothing yet is aware of everything as it is. This awareness is within me, as well as outside of me. It permeates everything; it has always been and will always be. It is the primary substance that exists around all things. It cannot cease to exist, neither does it get old; it is untouchable yet touches everything. It can only be recognized by acknowledgment through its own awareness of itself around you and accepted as that which you are, a part of it. As long as you live apart as individualized separate consciousness, which is the common mind-set, it appears hidden from your conscious awareness, though it is with you and around you at all times. Yet time has no effect upon it. This analogy is somewhat fitting: consider fish, who are born in water; they are not aware of the water, it is the primary substance, always there surrounding them, giving them being.

Align with the Divine

As we learn to align with the divine, we all will be fine. The definition of *fine* includes the following: free from impurity, excellent, very well, to become pure or clear. Just as an automobile must be properly aligned for travel, so must we be for our journey. In addition, if we fail to be aligned properly with the divine, our lives become impure and cloudy; we just cannot seem to figure out what the problem is, why our happiness seems so short-lived and sorrows follow us like shadows.

Delete the Devil

I am in the lunchroom at work; there is a person whose lunch box is sitting on the table. This thought was presented to my mind: "Put a bunch of spiders in his lunch box." I said, "Delete that." Instead put love in his lunch box, so that when he opens it he is greeted by love, not fear. My friends, it is just that simple. We can overturn the evil with good; we can overcome what we call the devil with God. We can defeat the illusion of hatred with the reality of love. We can overcome our fear-based lower self with our love-based higher self. We can delete the evil with love.

Now I Live

Being a man of immortal dimensions eliminates the mortal dimensions I once died in. I have survived death's dimension of mortality. I live now!

The Ax to Death and Tax

There is an old saying that is a fallacy: "There are two things you can be sure of, death and taxes." It is true they have created a tax for nearly everything. They will tax you to death. And in the mortal dimension, they have a death tax. They may tax me, but they will never tax me to death. I will take the "t" from their tax and make an ax and chop down their death and tax.

Are You Dead Asleep?

The noise of the world is also the snore of the world's largest sleep inn. You can witness sleep walkers and sleep talkers, sleep teachers and sleep preachers. This world is a graveyard, a cemetery. The word *cemetery* comes from the Greek, which means large dorm where many people are sleeping. It makes sense that Jesus the Christ once told a man to let the dead bury the dead. When you are asleep you know nothing, just as the dead, for that is what it appears you are. Well, until you rise up the next day.

Unreality

When someone is sleeping, they move very little. They are not dangerous; however, when they are dreaming or in a nightmare, you have to be careful. They will hit or kick you, talking all kind of gibberish. I have witnessed people sleep walking, talking, and eating. They believe what they are experiencing in the dream state. Perhaps humanity is reacting to the nightmare we call life, running wildly in fear from that which is not real.

Waking Up

Having left this world of illusion behind, shedding tears because you are still there, I will come for you, and be with me you shall indeed. Once you enter the kingdom, looking back you cannot fit back in the illusion, for you believe in it no more.

Illusions

When we believe in illusions, they become powerful; and when we do not believe in them, we find they are nothing. In this we find that the power lies in our ability to believe. Therefore, let us be very selective when, where, and into what we apply our power. This power is God-given, so put your power in the truth, which is God, and not into illusions, which are nothing.

The Garden of Roses

Was Jesus black, white, red, yellow, or brown? Jesus was whatever we are as humanity; he represented unity, not division. Jesus was Christ, Son of God expressed in human form. Roses differ in color and size; it is their fragrance, which cannot be seen yet can be smelled, that we love so well. In contrast Christ is the fragrance and the color of humanity; the thorns of a rose represent humanity's cruel side, which causes pain though we be so beautiful. If only we become the Christ again, we shall wear the crown of thorns no more.

The Great Depression

Humanity's depression is death! There is something in us that disagrees with death, for when death extends its invitation, see how we decline; we call an ambulance, we ask for prayer, we resist death. We do not like it, we fight it like the enemy that it is, we run from it, we try and hide from it, hoping that it will not find us. Yet in life we find love, happiness, hope, and dreams. The last enemy to be destroyed is death, setting us free from the great depression.

Nothing to Die for, Everything to Live for

You must see the Christ in those who have not seen the Christ within themselves. You cannot hurt that which you are; however, you can help those who have nothing to die for and everything to live for.

Overcoming Death

I see humanity running from death, but death cannot be outrun; it must be overcome. We cannot hide from death, for it eventually seeks us out, hunts us down, and, like a deadly sniper bullet, takes us out. We must tell death it has no place in us; we shall one day repeat the words of I Corinthians, 15:55 (KJV): "O death, where is thy sting? O grave, where is thy victory?" Like a hornet whose stinger has been removed, it is no longer to be feared. No more running, no more hiding from its terrible pursuit. Instead feel the power of Christ's immortality as your own.

* * I Am * *

I thrive, I live. I am from another place and, I would say, time. However, where I am from, there is no time.

True Freedom

The illusion does not want to let anyone go free. But who the Son sets free is free indeed. Sun is Son is powerful light, light eliminates darkness, and darkness binds the mind to believe in illusions. The enlightened mind sees the reality that Christ is light. Light is reality, the consciousness of God in action.

Being Awake

When someone is asleep at the wheel of life, you may feel compelled to awaken them. However, you cannot possibly tell them that you are awake. How can one who is asleep possibly know that you are awake? Only those who are awake can know those who are awake. And the ones who are awake know the ones who are still asleep. The sleeper never knows that they were asleep until they are fully awake.

Progression

We have come a long way in a short amount of time, or we have come a short way in a long amount of time. How is your progression?

Ascending

I am yet ascending!

* * I Am I * *

I am one with my human self.

~ *Spirit's Poetry* ~

Spirit is a new beginning if I choose it to be, where nothing of the past has power over me. People may say this and people may say that, but nothing can affect the present moment, that's a fact. Today is a new day never seen before; every thought, word, and deed is spirit ever more. Old things are passed away; behold, everything is new. Dark, menacing skies suddenly turn blue. The moment I decide today is new for me, spirit unfolds its power to be all I'm meant to be.

Chapter 7

~ CONTEMPORARY ~

You will see the effects of these thoughts in your life as you become aligned with them, as they are absorbed into your consciousness, changing the way you see the world. Those who use these powerful thoughts will change the world, and as the world changes, so will the people. We are all interconnected; every thought, word, and action brings with it a response, a reaction. If we are wise, we will choose carefully our thoughts, as well as our words and actions. We affect each other in a positive way, or we infect each other in a negative way. We are all existing simultaneously as individuals, yet we exist as one organism in our modern world; we cannot escape our oneness with one another, because we are one another, just appearing as different versions of the one. I share my light that others may see their light; within the concept lies the reality that we are one.

Life

Life is not about our petty desires or our individual pursuits of happiness. Life is the toad hiding in the garden under the zucchini leaves; life is the weeds that invade and attempt to overtake the garden. Life is not the new car, the new home, or the lost ring. Life is the cicada singing its song to attract a mate in the evening. Life is you and me trying to make a life that already is.

Gratitude

You will discover the secret to an awesome attitude as you live each moment with gratitude.

Evil in a Nutshell

Who or what is evil? We have been told that the love of money is the root of all evil. Does that imply that if there were no money, there could be no evil? Or that before there was such a thing as money, there was no evil? Why is it okay to say that I love the dress, or I love pizza, or any number of things that money buys, yet we feel if we love the money that affords us the experience, we have entered the domain or root of evil? This splits us in two. Now consider this: "The lack of love is the root of all evil." Do you feel a sense of clarity and oneness? Everything has its opposite: hot and cold, high and low, big and small, etc. The opposite of love would be evil/hate. If we reverse the spelling of *love* we get *evol* = evil, which is also the word *live* spelled backwards. The opposite of love is also fear and hatred. No one fears love; however, everyone fears evil. Living life in fear and hatred would be evil in a nutshell.

Broken Tears

When tears within my head fall down like rain from the clouds in the heavens of my mind, I understand the tears of a broken heart, when the one you shared love with has left you alone with your tears. They don't see your tears, and even if they did, those tears are yours, not theirs. You must wipe them dry and not drown in them.

No One Grows for You

There is no one that can grow for another; we each must grow in our own consciousness, and consciousness is what we are.

For Better or for Worse

It can be better if we decide to make it better; it can be worse if we decide to make it worse.

Adult Lessons

I think when an adolescent is going through adolescence, it prepares them for adult lessons. But I don't think they learn adult lessons until they are no longer an adolescent.

Face Life, Face Lift

If you need a face lift start facing life with love and turn that frown upside down.

The "P" Button

If we press the panic button, we experience all that comes with panic. If we press the peace button, do you suppose that we can experience peace?

Misperceptions

When I was a kid hearing the evening news reporting about guerrilla warfare in the jungles of Vietnam, I thought that gorillas were jumping out of trees and tearing the soldiers apart. I thought,

What a mess. They have to fight off dangerous gorillas plus the enemy.

My little cousin Wilson was watching TV and shouted, "Mom, Mom, come look at this!" His Mom ran from the kitchen to see what the urgency was, only to find him pointing at a snail on TV. She said, "What is it!" Wilson said, "Look, Mommy, the snail has a penis on his head." Wilson had interpreted the erect eyes of the snail as a penis.

Another time Wilson pointed at an airliner high in the sky and said, "Mom they shrunk the plane." Yet another time, Wilson was watching a TV commercial about women's jeans. He asked, "Mom, does that butt come with those jeans?"

Driving a Thought

We share our life with thoughts; the thoughts we think create our world. Think about it: we are driving Henry Ford's thought, we are dressed in thoughts, and we sit down on a thought (the couch). We are totally experiencing thoughts of individuals and the collective consciousness of humanity manifested in all the things perceived via our five senses. Starbucks was a thought; we drink our coffee from a thought that we call a coffee cup.

The Dream Thing

People with big dreams do big things. People with small dreams do small things. People with bad dreams do bad things People with good dreams do good things. People with no dreams do no thing.

Saving the Satisfaction of Spending

With most people, the more they make the more they spend. And for other people, the more they make, the more they save. My motto: Money spent cannot be saved, and money saved cannot be spent. So don't be afraid to save.

Now Understand That

Understanding comes with understanding that understanding comes with understanding. Now understand that understanding comes with understanding that?

Catching a Plane

When you find yourself running like you have to catch a plane, you might as well slow down. No one has ever caught a plane. Trust me. It's too big and too fast.

The Comfort Zone

When you get out of your comfort zone, you may find that you are now actually comfortable.

Reversed Evolution in Reverse

While in Orlando, Florida, I would notice these miniature dinosaurs watching me. As I would reach for them, they would run and hide. That is when I realized that I was now huge, like the dinosaurs, and the ancient dinosaurs had been reduced in size to tiny lizards. Reversed evolution in reverse.

Mind for Sale

It has been said that a mind is a terrible thing to waste, and that you should use your head for more than a hat rack. For those who have found no reason to constructively use what is in their heads, perhaps they should place an ad on eBay that says "Mind for Sale, Never Used."

Catching Game

My mother is like a lioness that ran down game to feed her seven cubs. Now that she is old and retired, my brother David stays by her side. One evening when she and I were talking on the phone, she said to me, "Hey, can I call you back? David just brought me something to eat." I replied, "Sure, enjoy!" Now the roles are reversed: she stays in the den while David runs down game for her in his Infiniti G35, yet unaware of how we mimic nature catching game.

Eye I Eye

Beauty is in the I of the beholder, and I am going to be holding you close to me, says the eye of the beholder.

Nice Fragrance

If you enjoy fine fragrances, you have to keep your nose clean.

Depth vs. Height

Just as we experience the depths of sorrow, there must also be heights of happiness to experience. One day while I visited my great uncle Bill, he said to me that he had no regrets, and that if you can get through the bad times, the good times are there just waiting on you. Then he said nothing. It sounded good enough to be true.

Low Self-Esteem.

I once told a coworker, whom I considered to be the best at plumbing, that he was the master plumber. His reply was that he was a "master asshole"; this person says, "The work leader is an asshole, a real piece of shit," and he was serious about it, yet called himself a master asshole. I do not refer to anyone as an asshole. True, everyone has one, but you don't have to be one. I think one asshole is enough for anyone, no matter how full of it they are.

More Low Self-Esteem

One day while at work, I heard someone say he was an asshole and didn't know shit! It struck me strangely, and I asked myself, *How can an asshole not know shit*? Do people really listen to what they are saying? Then one guy said to another guy, "You're an asshole," and the other guy said, "No, I'm a perfect asshole."

Dream on Sleeper

A dreamer talks in his sleep, so dismiss his gibberish. When he awakens, he will make more sense. While sleeping he dreams and believes the dream he's in to be real.

The Green Beings

As I observe the plant life, the green beings among us that grace our lawns, lend us their shade, and soften our homes with their greenery, I think they watch us, aware at all times. The life in green a witness to everything, they see our wars, blood spilled upon the grass, dripping off the leaf. Ancient trees and jungles have seen our travels; the bushes and trees around our homes watch families come and go. They remain a silent witness; they do not interfere. We think they cannot see or hear; oh, but they can! Speak to them, caress them, and be amazed.

Piss on Everyone!

I was driving behind a guy in a pickup truck. On the back window was written, "Piss on everyone." I used my new perspective and said to myself, *Well, he doesn't discriminate*, but I also thought, *What a sad life*. Then I said, "Maybe he's dyslexic and meant that everyone pisses." The bottom line: it's the lower vibration he's sending into the boomerang world.

I'm Proud to Be an American

I heard a worldly discussion on television in which Iran's new leader was described as a wolf in sheep's clothing. If Iran is a wolf in sheep's clothing, would it be fair to say America is a grizzly bear in wolf's clothing?

The Rights

Lets talk about rights: we had to fight for civil rights, women's rights, the right to plead the Fifth, rights to bear arms, rights for an abortion, human rights, the Bill of Rights, animal rights, farmers' rights, property rights, political party rights, union rights, employees' rights, employers' rights, corporate rights, prisoner rights, patient rights, other countries' rights, religious rights, parental rights, government rights, gay and lesbian rights, rights to your rights.

Laugh a Little!

The way things enter our understanding sometimes leads to a misunderstanding. I have seen the following in the newspaper: Professional Engineer wanted. Well who would want an *un*professional engineer? Seasoned firewood: What is it seasoned with? Paprika, salt and pepper? Garage sale: Is this saying the house is not for sale, garage only? Boxer for sale: Now, who would buy a boxer what are you supposed to do after you buy him, use him as your sparring partner?

Good

Smile because it feels good, it looks good, and it is good. When you look in the mirror, start smiling at the one looking back at you. Trust me, they will smile back every time.

Got to Give

It's not what you can get; it's what you can give. It's not what you got, it's that you can keep on giving. That's why you've got it ... to give.

To Be or Not to Be

Concerning things desired, if it is to be, then so be it, and if not, then so be it not.

In the Beginning

Happiness can begin with a smile; therefore, remember to smile at yourself and others in the beginning, and you will be happy in the end.

The Smile

A smile counts; it costs you nothing yet is worth more than all the money you could ever count. My prayers are with you; be blessed where it counts. Give yourself a smile for me, and I will give myself a smile for you. A smile from the heart expressed on the face and seen in the eyes is silent; our smiles speak without words. Can you hear a smiling heart? Our inner smile no one sees until we release it upon our face. If you know that God is with you, smile! If you have ever smiled yet think God cannot possibly be with you, then smile and think again! Smile! You are not on *Candid Camera*, but I have you in my lens. When you smile, you bless yourself and the world.

Random Acts of Kindness

What makes a person decorate someone's tree with toilet paper or set a paper bag full of dog shit by their front door, set it on fire, ring the doorbell, and run? Such a person is obviously out of control, with too much time on their hands and desperate for the wrong type of attention. What makes them feel good is making others feel bad. What they're missing is the magic formula in random acts of kindness, the acts that make everyone feel the good feelings that accompany kindness.

The Body Manual

If you know not how a car works and the necessary maintenance to keep it operating at peak performance, you will be buying a new car much sooner than necessary. It is not that way with your organic vehicle, your body. If you neglect it and wreck it, that's it; there is no replacement. Study your owner's manual, follow it, and live a healthier, longer life. Our food should be our medicine; we shouldn't have to take medicine because of our food.

Changing Your Mind

It's okay to change your mind, because it's your mind that creates change.

With Certainty

We believe in our abilities; we believe in our inabilities with certainty.

More or Less

Adding to something that needs no more makes as much sense as subtracting something from something that needs more.

Being Free

It feels good being free from the lust for women, allowing one's mind to see them as the mother of our race.

Flow

The palm tree in the storm bends with the wind, while the kelp in the ocean goes with the flow. We are better off in life's storms when we also go with the flow.

To Give

Is it possible that we only get what we give? If you need compassion but you hide it from me, you hide it also from yourself.

Kurt M. Jordan

Believing the Dream

If you live within the dream, you die within the dream, because you believe the dream is real. Dreams are powerful illusions when we believe in them; when we don't, they are nothing.

Higher Thought

A mountain has two sides, each with opposing views, but at the summit all is clearly seen and understood.

Some Cannot!

Some cannot see; therefore, I overlook their blindness. Some cannot hear; therefore, I overlook their deafness. Some cannot walk; therefore, I overlook their lameness. I do this by loving them as though they were whole, and so as I am they shall be.

On and Off

On the scene you do your thing; off the scene you are no longer seen.

Give What Matters

It is not what you get in this life but what you give that matters. I shall not want; I shall give; and in giving I shall have, and I shall not want.

Unhurtable

Now unhurt I am able.

Its Thoughts Are Lies

The devil is a lie. The name is *lived* spelled backward, which is death, is evil, which is *live* spelled backward. A lie is not true; neither is a devil.

Lies are spawned in darkness; falseness flees from the light. Do not hold its hand, do not heed its voice, do not take the tempting bait; the hook is twice sharpened, and it will turn your life backward, starting with your mind. It cares for no one; it is the absence of love. Can such a character exist?

Playing House

One should not play house unless one is able to pay the bills.

Nothing Less, Nothing More

Women are just women, nothing less and nothing more. Same with men.

Lonely

To be lonely translates into feeling: L = love, O = only, N = never, E = ever, L = loves, Y = you. The pain of loneliness can be quenched only with love, and love always loves you. To be lonely is a feeling that you need to love and be loved; when this is not the case, you feel lonely.

Trust Is Earned

If children cannot trust their parents, it creates false trust in them, which may follow them their whole life through.

Compassion

A father should have compassion on his little children.

A Beautiful Thought

Beauty from within never fades with time, while outer beauty fades away every time.

Which Part?

You are either part of the problem or part of the solution.

True Credit

When a person tries to make right what they did wrong, that is credited on their character account.

Success

Your success is my success, your failure my failure. When we fail to love, we experience failure. Love is successful, for it never fails to love.

The Kurteous Prayer

Be my strength that I may be strength for others. Be my bridge that I may be a bridge for others. Be my love that I may be love for others. Then I will be a strong bridge of love for all.

Food for Thought

Something other than the world must feed your mind. You see, the world is a farce, and without that something else, you become part of the farce. In this book I offer an alternative way of thinking, a fresh perspective, a way of servicing your mind: out with the old, in with the new. We are living in a time when your mind must feed on something other than the world.

Why?

Poverty is a way of life for billions. Prosperity is a way of life for few. Poverty begins in the mind and can end in the mind. Prosperity in the mind can end the poverty of the mind.

Having No Sense

Sometimes you don't have any sense, but you don't know you don't have no sense because you don't have no sense and the things you do only make sense to you. There once was a terrible hurricane coming. The warning to get out of harm's way came from a man who went to a home with a light on. He knocked on the door, and a frightened woman with two kids answered the door. The man said, You have to leave now, this hurricane is a big one. She said, "I can't; my husband won't let us leave; he's in the bathtub; he heard it's the safest place for us to be." The husband shouted from the tub to close the door, that they would be fine. The next day, after the storm passed, the man went back to check on the couple with the kids. The house and the family were nowhere to be found.

Tension and Peace

Tension in the mind will manifest as tension in the body. Peace in the mind will release tension from the body. A peaceful mind will manifest as

peace in the body. Lust in the mind will manifest as tension in the body, while love in the mind will manifest peace in the body.

Primitive Culture

A primitive culture has an inability or unwillingness to solve differences without violence. We are that primitive culture.

Consciousness

Consciousness cannot be observed, yet scientists think they can observe what we are thinking by use of electronic instruments. Consciousness cannot be observed.

Abundance!

Understanding abundance and the law that governs it would emphasize that there is no lack, only abundance. Therefore, lack would be an illusion made up by the minds of those who believe in lack over abundance. This brings us to what we believe in, which has actually become our subconscious belief. We either believe in abundance or we believe in lack, and this will work itself out into our lives.

"I Thought"

We often say, "I thought I wanted it." Why did we think we wanted it? You thought, and so you did. It is our thoughts that gets us started wanting in the first place.

Overtime

A thought about overtime: when you think about overtime, it may bring to mind working beyond your normally scheduled hours for an employer, or maybe a basketball game that continues in order to break a tie. However, you either build your life over time, or you destroy your life over time, and then time is over.

Difference

Skilled or unskilled?

Illusions

Illusions play a big part here on earth. If you do not overcome illusions, you become convinced they are real and confused by them. An illusion is an ill use on the mind, which prevents us from seeing the truth accurately. In such cases we are often deluded with illusions.

People Handle with Care

It's not how you handle others but how you handle yourself while handling others that makes the difference.

Happiness and Depression

Happy people are happy about being happy, as depressed people are depressed about being depressed.

The Stare

We find it incredibly easy to stare for hours at a television full of strangers. Yet we find it incredibly difficult to look one another in the face for more than a minute. It seems we can stare if we don't care; but if we care, we fear the stare.

Ninety Degrees

Changes perception.

Time and Memory

Time gets lost in memories, and memories get lost in time.

Smelling Bee

It has been said that in life you should stop and smell the roses; however, while smelling be sure you don't get a bee sting in your nose.

Mother

While I was in my mother's womb, she lived for us both.

I'm Your Pusher Man

Patients are told to listen to their doctors, and doctors are waiting to hear from their patients. Our doctors are practicing on patients, and the patients have to be patient, while the drug-pushing kingpins use mass marketing in magazines and television commercials that pushes the public to push their doctors to give them the drugs that potentially can cause all manner of problems, including death, while the patients are expected to be patient while they gamble with their lives as the drug pusher's profits go through the roof and the drug-dealing doctors write prescriptions for the nervous patients who purchase the drugs from pharmacies who give the drugs to the patients losing patience with a dangerous dope game, while the doctor hopes to not lose a patient from the potentially fatal side effects that the drug-pushing pharmaceutical giants have advertised to patients that they should go to their doctors and ask about getting the drugs that were engineered to help their condition.

Illogical

We should not kill ourselves and try to live; neither should we try to live by killing ourselves. Yet that happens every day, from our improper eating habits, lack of exercise, and smoking, and the list goes on. This is illogical.

A Drop of Life

Since governments can drop death from the sky, can they not drop life from the sky? Why are death and destruction dropped over life and love? For some reason we are primitive in the use of our technology.

The Highway of Life

When I'm driving on the highway, I prefer to not drive behind a semi. It's an obstacle that I can't see around. I want to see where I'm going and what lies ahead. On the highway of life, space and time are obstacles like the semi. I cannot see around them, and I want to see where I am going and what lies ahead. I would need to travel at the speed of light to pass the vehicles of space and time, or become one with the light, eliminating them both.

Good Investment

Your smile is an asset that you can invest in without a dime, has a guaranteed return on investment, takes no time, and makes your face and others' shine.

Home Owner's Thought

Most people who think they are homeowners are actually home owers.

The Advantage

I do not take advantage of anyone; instead, I choose to give them the advantage.

King of Confidence

Self-confidence should be a natural state of being. If a lion had no confidence, it would starve. The lion does not doubt its ability to capture prey; therefore, it eats. Lions don't know what doubting is. To doubt is unnatural. When we doubt our own abilities, we starve the king of confidence within ourselves.

Walls

We must see beyond the wall, or the wall will become our prison; there is another side. The wall can represent anything that would hold us back from reaching our maximum positive potential.

Dancing with the Stars

Movie stars are paid enormous sums of money for what each of us does every day: act! They serve as reflections of humanity, that's all. I would rather be a star than a movie star. The shine is much brighter, it lasts much longer, and my name is written in the heavens for all to see, not on the ground for all to walk upon, especially if you get in trouble.

The Goal Is!

Goal-less thinking goals nowhere.

Push the Button?

The world we live in moves fast, from transportation to computers. We have learned well to use the delete button. However, we cannot delete so quickly the problems of the world. We must slow down; we are going way too fast on this superspeed highway.

An Observation

Observe everything, judge nothing; judgment is meaning less, not more.

Kurt M. Jordan

What Is Looking at You?

A person looks at you with their consciousness, not with their eyes. Though they work together, the eye cannot see without the consciousness.

War on Wellness?

Humanity has been fighting sickness ever since it caused us to suffer and die. A strange statement I will make is that some people are actually fighting wellness. Tell me, what is wrong with us? For when we become sick, we seek to become well, and when we are well, we do things that cause us to become sick.

Success versus Failure

You cannot be successful with thoughts of failure; neither can you be a failure with thoughts of success. You can succeed in failure, or you can fail to succeed

Beauty and Joy

Flowers and butterflies delicate and beautiful; one on the wing, the other on a stem, they express beauty and joy to all.

Of Course

Can you become younger than yesterday? How about smarter? How about lovelier?

Thoughts about Humanity

If you can admire and love the great variety of flowers, you can admire and love the great variety of human beings. The two share so much in common: they come in all shapes, sizes, and colors; they grow and bloom; they wither and are gone, and if not for the seed they planted in the earth, you'd not know they were ever here. Man sows his seed in woman, which brings forth little children who remind us in their innocence of flowers, which we all love.

The Humane Society

We, being civilized savages, condemn the dog fighters; we call them inhumane for pitting two dogs against each other while spectators watch the battle until one wins over the other. How can we call ourselves civilized, a humane society, when our most intelligent heads of state pit man against man in what we call war against so-called enemies? If it's inhumane to watch dogs rip and tear one another to pieces, how is it humane to be a spectator of war, as men kill one another by the thousands? I heard a World War II veteran say with much emotion, "There is no glory in war, only gory." Is there a difference between dog fighters and human fighters; are we really a humane society?

Ignorance

Racism is ignorance at its worst. It's a disease that we have accepted. Like cancer it eats us from within. However, we don't accept cancer when it shows its ugly head; it's an enemy we seek to destroy. We change our diets, go under the knife, take chemo treatments, lose our hair, and donate money to find a cure. We wouldn't infect our children, family, or friends with cancer. Then why would we infect them with the cancerous disease of racism, unless we are ignorant?

Word Power!

Our words carry power when we speak them; they can cut like a knife or heal like a balm; they can lift our spirits and cause our souls to soar; or they can crush our spirits and scorch our souls. Here are some words to consider: I hate this! I hate that!

Let me say that I hate nothing, for I have no time or place for hate in my life. I chose to eliminate it from my vocabulary. All I need is love, not love and hate, so hate has to go, because I have power to let it go.

I used to say "I am tired," but now I choose to say "I shall rest," for whatever I say, I am giving myself permission to experience more of. With this understanding, I can use words to promote or demote, to bless or curse: it's up to me.

So let us be careful of the words we use and how we express ourselves; our words are as important as our thoughts.

I have noticed also that people lash out with words like "f__k you" or "goddamn you." We can use our word power differently by saying, "forgive you" or "God bless." We have the power to do this; do we have the courage, and do we have the heart? Instead of "hell, yes," we can say "heavens, yes." With these constructive words, we can free ourselves.

Understanding Our Existence

Everyone is here on earth looking at one another, trying to see who has the understanding about our existence. No one will ask, but I can see it in their actions, I can see it in their eyes. This I understand.

How It Is

It is not how you see it or how someone else sees it; it is how it is, period, untouched by the individual or collective opinion.

Just Remember

A little kindness and a little respect will go a very long way.

Decisions

When you must decide, your decision should be for the highest good in your life and not just for the moment that it seems good, because then it will be good only for the moment.

Racial Segregation

Means get out and stay away from us. It meant something is wrong with you, when in fact there was nothing wrong at all. However, there is actually something wrong with racists by reason of their racism.

Fantasy

Is like taking your mind and heart on a journey that your body cannot follow.

The Future Present

What the future holds no one knows, but the present is definitely for you.

Season of Loneliness

There is a difference in summer and winter. There is a difference in spring and fall. Though the seasons change, loneliness can make them all feel the same.

Enemy or Friend of Me

Time is our enemy and time is our friend, for no sooner have we started, it says, *Now is your end*. Time lets us grow and then time lets us go. Time helps us be the star, then time says no more. Time lifts us up and then time tears us down. Time makes us happy and then time makes us sad. Time treats us good, then time treats us bad. Time is an illusion we wish we never had.

Ashtrays

One day ashtrays will be obsolete, for in that day humanity will have risen beyond the smoke that clouds our vision and destroys our health.

We Make Things

Things do not make me; I make things. What is a ring without my finger, and what is a home without me to live in it? What is a car without a driver, or clothes without someone to wear them? What is money without a buyer?

Recipe for Success

It is not enough to just have the recipe for a cake: you need the ingredients too. Likewise, you can have all the ingredients and lack the recipe. So it is with personal success.

Dream in Reality

There is a big difference between a dream and reality. Reality is the way it is. A dream is the way we wish it to be. Reality is not a dream! A dream is not reality; sometimes it becomes a reality. But until it does, it is just a dream in reality.

Better Act Better

When attacked from the back, there is no need to attack back, when attacked from the front, there is no need to attack from the front. When people act out of attack mode, you'd better act better.

When You Move

Move in confidence or do not move at all. If you must move, move in confidence.

Mental Mess

When we were infants we pooped on ourselves; as if all was well. As adults, we poop in our minds and walk around as if all is well. Toxic thoughts and images too often produce our toxic actions. When we decide that our mind is not the place to poop, we will no longer be in a mental mess.

Tyranny Must End!

We are not grapes or oranges, yet throughout history there have been and continue to be those among us who have squeezed the very life juices from others. Driven by their lust for wealth, blinded by greed and pursuit for pleasure, they discard the souls of others like grape skins after the press, like orange peels when making juice. They took land from others through what was called colonization, squeezed the precious resources from the land, squeezed the souls of many.

Human Capability

Humanity is capable of doing great evil; humanity is more capable of doing great good. Which will you do?

The Garden

This is my observation in the garden of eating. We plant the seed, and God gives the increase. Then the rabbit, groundhog, and insect give the decrease in the garden of eating.

Judge less

The end of judgment is the beginning of love, yet who am I to judge in the name of love? We seem to have an insatiable appetite for judging others. God is the only one who can give righteous judgment in love. I often err in my judgments; therefore, I need not judge often. Who am I to make a judgment of life? It's that judging appetite again. Our prejudices against those who appear different from us isn't necessary at all. We just have to love them. They're just talking heads and we're taking heads when we judge them instead of love them.

Regrets

If you don't want regrets, keep looking forward, and don't look back.

What Happened?

Ever notice how adults are portrayed in sitcoms and movies? Men as sexual idiots, and women as sex objects, while children appear wiser than both? Men and women have a respectable and meaningful position in life, and it's not to be idiots. If you watch enough of this behavior, you may become a carbon copy of some writer's twisted imagination.

To Know

To know is to ask someone who knows.

Childhood Trauma Creates Adulthood Drama

Certain physical and emotional events have happened to some of us that almost killed us or wounded us severely. I say childhood trauma creates adulthood drama. Many people are acting out of what traumatized them during childhood; these events become trapped in the body, suppressed in the mind. They can be released through certain movements combined with sound and breathing. I could feel trauma leaving my body, that is when I knew what was happening and it can happen for you. If trauma remains in the body, all sorts of negative conditions can arise.

The You Turn Allowed

A dead-end job, relationship, or lifestyle is just that. It is dead, same as dead-end thinking; it has no life in it for you. It is like trying to go somewhere and somehow ending up on a dead-end road. You literally cannot go any farther; there is no more road to travel. At this point you must make a U-turn. In order to make a U-turn, you have to turn yourself around and focus on a positive direction. The most important U-turn that one can make is in one's thinking, for it is the thoughts of a person that determine which direction they will go in life. A dead end leaves you feeling dead in the end. There is no sign on the highway of life that says *no you turn allowed.*

Be the Best You Can Be

The government solicits young people to join the army. If we had a higher concept of the army, we would recognize that you are me as the greatest army in the world it would raise our consciousness. I can't kill you, because you are me. When we look at another person we are seeing a different version of ourselves.

Mother's Love

Without our mother, we were all doomed as infants; our fathers couldn't feed us, for they had no milk. Therefore, our Mother's Day celebration comes down to the breast we suckled and the love she gave us.

Common Sense

One reason some people are successful is that they positioned themselves for success.

Never Quit

One should never quit trying to quit a bad habit.

The Power to Be!

We have been stupid; now let's be smart. We have been ignorant; now let's be educated. We have been weak; now let's be strong. We have been cold; now let's be warm. We have been stiff; now let's be flexible. We have been poor; now let's be wealthy. We have been wrong; now let's be right.

Want Means Lack

The statement "I want it" indicates the lack of it.

The Dog Consciousness

I hear and I see men talking and they say, "Piss on you." I see bumper stickers of a boy with a smirk pissing on a brand of truck or pissing on Osama bin Laden. I think men's minds are becoming like male dogs who relieve themselves on trees and other objects. Man is not a dog, yet he is acting out dog consciousness instead of god consciousness. A dog will not be sexually monogamous but will instead mate with a female and then go to other females, leaving their offspring to fend for themselves. There is no loyalty, no responsibility. Men who do this are acting out of dog consciousness instead of god consciousness. Women are calling themselves bitches nowadays, and yet they say they want to be treated and respected. People with a low-grade mentality say "Kiss my ass," which is something that dogs do. Something has to change in their consciousness.

You Are Your Word

Your words about yourself become your truth about yourself, so always be aware of what you tell yourself about yourself, and make it something positive.

Movie Time

My life is a movie, and you are in it!

Dream Projections

Kurt the man whose dream came true. No, whose dreams ended and reality came through. One awakened from sleep. Whatever you believe to be real in a dream seems real to you, even though its not. Take, for instance, a new tile floor that you think looks nice; you project what you believe about niceness into the floor. Yet years later, you find the same floor unattractive. By projecting your new thought belief into the tile, it is no longer nice. Each time you have decided by your personal belief what the tile will be, nice or not nice. It is only your belief that makes it so. According to your belief, so be it unto you, for nothing comes to a sleeper except a dream or a nightmare, yet neither one is real, unless you prefer to make it that way.

Real Things

The only thing that is real is real.

No Half Stepping

Never half step when you can take a whole step to change your whole life for the better.

Leading the Masses

The reason the masses are misguided and misinformed is that the guides are also misguided and misinformed. The time for the true guides and the truly informed to arise and lead the way is now!

Ain't Means Ain't

I was listening to my brother talk about the depressing, messy life he had created, when he said, "I ain't shit." I told him, "you are right. You ain't shit; you are somebody." The lesson here is to speak only the truth about yourself and understand the truth that you speak.

The One Mystery

Life has many mysteries, and we are one of them.

Fooled Again?

The illusion is whatever is not true yet convinces us every time that it is true.

To Be

Highly skilled or unskilled at anything makes a big difference.

Time to Change

Time seems to play a trick on us; look at us change.

The Art of Business

I am perfecting the art of minding my own business ... you should try it sometime.

Understanding the Enemy

The world is not your enemy; not understanding it is your enemy.

Emotion

Emotion is energy in motion, our feelings generated by thought.

You Turn

You cannot make a U-turn until you decide to turn.

The Cost of Time

"There is just not enough time!" Let me sell you some time; if you have the money, I have the time. How much does time cost? No one knows. Nevertheless, there is plenty of it, so much no one can count it; time can be neither packaged nor preserved, but it can be wasted.

Climbing the Ladder

There is a hidden ladder in the basement of your mind; you can find it if you know where to look. Once you find it, you must climb it. Do not be afraid; the ladder is very sturdy. You cannot fall off of this ladder. It's the ladder in your mind that leads to higher consciousness.

Dreams Come True

Helping people make their dreams come true is a dream come true, so always help people make their dreams come true.

Finding Your Element

It is important to find one's element. A whale in the middle of the ocean is so graceful, while a human in the middle of the ocean will perish. A beached whale will perish, while a human on the beach is safe and happy.

The Have Not

Helping people who have not, to have now.

Cannot Afford It

We can no longer afford to be poor, as though we ever could afford it. We can't afford to be in poor health; it costs too much. We can't afford to be poor in spirit; the flesh has profited us nothing. We can't afford to die; we must live!

We Live!

Eat, drink, and be merry, for tomorrow we live!

Healthy Thought

As exercise keeps the body in shape, educating oneself about positive things keeps the mind in shape.

Reason

Find no reason to criticize, yet find every reason to love.

Mind Thought

You see through your mind, and you write through your mind.

Not True

One day I realized that I did not want to believe anything that was not true; therefore, neither do I want to believe anything about myself that is not true.

The Condom

One day while jogging I saw a used condom in the parking lot. Disgusting. Next time I jogged there it was, just as disgusting. The one who tossed it is never going to get rid of that used condom. I snagged it with a twig and tossed it into the weeds. When we can take action, we should. Now no one has to see the used condom in the parking lot.

Nothing

If you are a do-nothing, you will do nothing.

Men Who Speak

I pay no attention to men who speak great words of nothingness, which are not great at all, who tomorrow are as dead as they are today.

Must

Assume nothing. Know everything you can.

Putting It into Perspective

What do we love and cherish more than power, money, sex, family, friends, possessions, food, and pets? How about our next breath? Think about it.

You Buy!

Anyone can buy something, but can you get anyone to buy from you? Therein lies the potential for prosperity.

Control

If you do not control sex, it will control you. If you cannot control money, it will control you too. If you cannot control your eating, you will get fatter and fatter and fatter.

Mental Garbage

The world is constantly sending images, words, and obscene suggestions to our minds; we are bombarded all day long with negative and unproductive material. We must dispose of this garbage just as we do from our homes. The content we keep in our minds is important; it will attract hummingbirds and butterflies or maggots and vultures.

Grant Us More

Our beauty does fade away like a wilting flower. What was is no more; aging is unmerciful as time devours our youthfulness. Perhaps it is all vanity, and surely life would grant us more if we sought more than vanity.

The Kind Mind

Your kindness is key. Be kind in your mind, and your actions will follow.

Mental Pretzel

There is no success in failure, unless one has succeeded in becoming a failure. There is no failure in success, unless one has failed because of one's success.

Rename Yourself

Take your name and use each letter to represent a positive word, and then live by your name. Example:

K = kind
U = understanding
R = rich
T = true

You may also extend your name or nature into a positive attribute.

Like Kurteous!

The Lemon Aid

We all may have heard the saying that when life gives you a lemon, make lemonade. What if you don't like lemonade? You can sell the lemonade to the thousands who do, and watch the lemon aid you.

A Thought for Sale

Stop, look, stare if you must, and see that everything you are observing is an out-picturing of an idea, a series of thoughts made manifest. Everything ever made for sale is actually thought for sale!

Fighting Men

When you fight a man, you find the boy, in order to beat the man. However, if the boy is as strong as the man is, you can't beat him.

Your Personal Power

There are certain things that are connected to your personal power.

They may be a certain color, sound, music, art, a word or affirmation, certain movements, a thought, a fragrance, scenery, an animal, or an object. Whatever it is that causes you to feel your best, that inspires you, that gives you that confident feeling, nail it down. Know what it is. Put it all together and walk out into the world with whatever your positive endeavor may be, and you will make a difference that day.

Be Efficient, Be Effective

When you become sure of yourself, you can be efficient and effective at what you do. When you are not sure of yourself, you tend be neither.

A Correct Thought

Onward and upward with forward thinking, for it will surely take me onward, upward, and forward!

Positive Focus

One need only to focus on a positive direction and follow through. The rest will be a great his-story or a great her-story of success.

The Last Thing to Think About

The last thing that you want to think about is something that you don't want to think about.

Space Beings

Funny observation about us earthlings: we are actually space beings who live in outer space, who travel in spaceships we call airplanes. We live within space suits made of skin, which over time get wrinkled and sag. There are no replacement suits: only one suit per person, and if it gets torn it can usually be sewn up to live in another day. If not, discard and the space being goes away.

Personal Progress

I have made thee to my liking, and I like what I have made, says the person satisfied with their personal progress.

Income Equals Outcome

Your income will determine your outcome, and it goes deeper than money, for if a person has few if any prosperous thoughts coming into his mind, his outcome will likely be poor.

The Top

I will see you at the top: this phrase insinuates where you are going and the expectation of not being there alone. You see, there is always room at the top; it's at the bottom where you find little room.

The Past

All photographs are of the past the moment they are taken. How interesting.

Solutions

Figure out the problem, and then proceed to correct it. The problem is the negative, the solution is the positive; when the two come together, it is a wonderful thing.

Positive Thought

Accentuate the positive!

Other Minds

I don't allow negative projections from other minds to project into my mind.

The Foolish Thought

I once heard a man gleefully say, "I'm a gambling fool!" How ironic.

Beyond Perception

Reaching people beyond their limiting perception of you will be a new breakthrough.

A Dog's Sense of Humor

I raised dogs for fifteen years. I worked for them, provided food and water for them, made kennels, gave shots, trimmed nails, walked with them, talked with them, brushed, petted, and praised them, picked up their poop, and bathed them. Who was the master, and who was the servant?

Almost There

Once you are almost there in your mind, you are almost there, and once you are there in your mind, you are there. Take a memory, which is a thought, and think about the time and place. You will notice that you are there instantaneously.

Diamonds

The diamond symbolizes that marriage can be the hardest relationship you will be in, and the most beautiful relationship. They say diamonds are forever and a girl's best friend, but diamonds end up in the pawnshop too.

Income Equals Outcome

Your income will determine your outcome, this applies to your mental diet not just your finances, and you need good incoming thoughts in order to have a good outcome in life. Your life is lived through your thoughts; your inner world is projecting this outer world we call life. Thoughts operate on this principle. Take a DVD movie, now place it in the DVD player; what you see is the projection of what was on the disc. If you don't like the movie, you press the eject button and replace it with one that is projecting what you want to see. These writings have the potential of injecting new thoughts and displacing old thoughts for a fresh new projection experience just waiting for you to behold.

Givers and Takers

The givers keep on giving, and the takers keep on taking.

The Blast of Time

Time is blasting away at us, trying to test what we are made of, blasting away at our faces, changing the landscape of our bodies. Changing who we thought we were. Time blasts us into dust. Yes, time wins over us.

The Same Difference

Everyone tries to be different yet ends up the same. If we get a tattoo to be different, we find that we become the same as everyone else who has a tattoo. If we wear saggy pants to be different, we become the same as everyone who is sagging. The way to be different is simple. Be the original individual that you are; there's only one unique you in the whole universe.

Self-Importance

We think it is important to be right, but it is more important to listen, learn, and understand. When you think you are right, and actually you are wrong, your thinking you were right was not important at all. When someone corrects your error, it is honorable to thank him or her, for now you will speak the truth in humility. In addition, when you are right and another is wrong, correct them if it is fitting, and go your way in humility.

Depression

I would define depression as the seemingly inability to let go of something depressing and move forward and upward in one's thoughts and emotions.

Cool Inside

We see people whom we consider to look cool, and perhaps they do, yet it is the person within that is cool, not just their appearance.

Think about It

A person leaves their thoughts on the earth in the form of something they have created and then goes away, never to be seen again. What they formed becomes a testament that they were here.

To Know

The whole thing is to know; you cannot deal with something that you do not know.

Origin of Greed

It is from the deepest emptiness of self that greediness and excess come.

The Mess

When one's sorrows exceed one's joy, one becomes a depressed mess.

Fear Not the Truth

We should not be afraid of the truth; it is the untruth that we believe that is frightening.

An Agent of Change

It is not enough to teach someone how to fish, nor is it enough to teach someone how to make money, but when you teach someone how to think, that person can become an agent of change.

Greetings with a Smile

Smiles are greetings without words, yet they speak for themselves.

Private Matters

In all matters considered private, and all matters of the body considered private, the most private of all are one's thoughts.

Because We Are Here

We are convinced there is something here for us, so we search all the days of our lives for love, for riches, for meaning, for something because we are here.

Now

Now thirty years from now will still be now. We cannot escape the now, because everything happens in it, whether it's the past, present, or future. The now is the permanent template of life.

But How?

Because the now is all the time!

Live Your Best Life

My best may be your worst, or your worst may be my best. We all have different abilities, talents, and gifts. They are as varied and numerous as we are. As long as you know you did your best and gave all you had to give, you have lived your best life.

"No Trespassing"

I have observed something quite strange in our humanity: we place signs on our properties that say "No Trespassing." What is the problem with someone walking across a field or on the outskirt of the woods that sends us into taking action against them? We run out to find what they are doing on our property, or we call the law. Yet if we see a herd of deer, a flock of geese, rabbits, raccoons, or almost any other creature, we have peace while they trespass on our property.

Open Minds Do See

Something is wrong in society that is worth noting. They say it is against the law to use fireworks in the city, but you may buy them. I saw a huge billboard that expressed the exhilaration of a woman in full glee at winning at the casino. What it did not show is the anguish one feels after losing money. Beer advertisements encourage us to live the "high life," but if you are caught living the "high life," you may be arrested for driving high. Have you noticed how advertisers use large print to sell you and then small print to deceive you? Open your mind and you will see.

Invest

The greatest investment is in oneself.

Using the Energy of Thought

When there is something that you are good at, you have certain energy behind it, a super confidence, and a doubt-free mind-set that causes you to move in the groove of success. It may be putting on your makeup or painting, it may be cooking meals or repairing things, it may be spelling or math. Whatever it is you know! When you are encountering something that you don't know, it's just the opposite. You seem to have no energy behind you, your confidence is low, and doubts can be high. Try taking the essence of the energy of the thing that you are good at doing, and transfer the energy essence into the thing you now desire to be good at doing.

Read My Thoughts and Live

Why do some people toss their lives away on a bad day, while others have a lives of hunger, one set of tattered, soiled clothes, are uneducated, homeless, and totally broke, yet do not toss their lives away? It must be the condition of their thoughts more so than the condition of their plight in life. I personally knew three people who tossed their lives away. If they could have read my thoughts, they might have gained a new perspective and chosen to live.

Mike Thought

My friend Mike said these words to me: "Now that I know better and I see better, I want better." I thought *Mike is right; he got it right.*

Inside Living Outside

We live on the inside, but we pay so much attention to the outside. People want to re sculpt their bodies, with liposuction, breast enhancements, penis enlargement, facelifts, tummy tucks, porcelain veneers, and hair transplants. These are fine, yet if we put more emphasis on re-sculpting our thoughts, we would live happier lives inside, instead of trying so hard to find a happier life on the outside.

The End of Desire

Of all the things desired in life, is the end of desire possible? I imagine it would come by total fulfillment, leaving nothing to be desired except desire, because desire seems to propel creation.

It Is the Thought That Counts

We follow our thoughts; where they go, we go. When you think of a good time past, present, or future, your thought takes you there; you see and feel the power of thought! There is an endless number and variety of thoughts to think. There are beautiful thoughts, peaceful thoughts, anxious thoughts, fearful thoughts. There are intimate thoughts, selfish thoughts, pitiful thoughts, low-down and dirty thoughts that will create a low-down and dirty situation, and there are higher thoughts that will give the thinker a higher situational advantage. There are unhealthy thoughts and unproductive thoughts, like "I'm going to get wasted," versus a healthier thought, like "I am going to have a nutritious dinner accompanied by a glass of wine." The thoughts you think can become your now or later experience. Behind the thought are your will and the ability to choose if you will act upon the thought. No crime can be committed without a preceding thought. Neither can one do a kind gesture without a preceding thought. As a thinker of thoughts, it is up to you which kind of thoughts you will consistently think, for this will be your making.

Haunting Regrets

If you could have one wish today, it would it be to wish my regrets away.

Life without Pain

I walk without pain and I live without pain. I love without pain because I have no pain. I laugh without pain and I sleep without pain, because a life without pain is a wonderful thing.

Skin Deep?

There is nothing like seeing the person behind the white skin, the black skin, the yellow skin, the red skin, the brown skin. Those who judge by the skin tend to be skin deep, and skin has no depth. Therefore, you must always look past the skin, for that is where each of us dwells, just beneath the skin.

You Cannot

You cannot change the desire of a person's heart.

A Redundant Thought

You do not know what you're missing if you don't know what you're missing.

PMS

Some women experience what is commonly known as PMS (premenstrual syndrome). And some men experience PMS as (power, money, and sex); think about it.

Remolding the Mind

In order to change our minds, we need to remold our thoughts, we need to rethink ourselves.

Pulling out All the Stops!

When we say we are pulling out all the stops, we think of trying hard, or trying to impress someone. I think what it really means is that anything that would stop us from being happy and successful must be pulled out of our consciousness.

Success and Failure

What defines success? Is it an abundance of money and material possessions? When you can look and not lust, I think you are successful. When you can forgive, forget, and keep on loving, you are successful. What defines failure? It is when material possessions and money possess you? It is when you cannot stop lusting and can't start forgiving.

The Wino's Creed

There is no end to wine, there's no end to time, and any wine anytime will be fine.

A Great Thought

Think great thoughts today, for great thoughts help make a great day.

You Give What You Got

Sometimes you give it all you got, and sometimes you got it all; you give.

Thought Attracts Thought

I thought her thoughts were attracting my thoughts. I thought I could feel her thoughts bumping into mine. I had never thought about thoughts doing such a thing, but thoughts are living energy, and they do get around.

The Movies of the Mind

All thoughts create images in the mind. We call this imagination; it is the little movie screen in your mind. We are to choose what we watch, but what we watch is a product of our thoughts. I do not try to control the outer world, but I do control my inner world of thoughts that produce the images in my mind. In order to produce a great movie in the mind, you will need great thoughts, and great thoughts produce greater movies outside the mind, the kind that we can live. In reality we are living projectors directing our own self-made movies for all to see.

Money and Self-Worth

Once you know that you are worth more than all the money you could ever work for, you will make money work for you. Remember, you make money, and money does not make you!

Lack and Having

Having a lack of self-confidence is one of the heaviest weights to carry around in life. While having a heavy self-confidence is lighter than a feather.

The World League to Free Women

This league is not sexist, anti-men, or a feminist movement. This league is about justice, fairness, respect, equality, and love. It is successful because its time has come. Its members are not limited to females, but are open for all who believe in its purpose and plan. The plan to free women who are under any type of bondage or domination can work if we all work toward this goal. Since the male of our species is the main perpetrator, I will focus briefly on men. The only power a man needs is over himself, period! As a male, it's his responsibility to protect and defend women and children. The world is a twisted place, but we have the power and ability to untwist and align with a divine purpose and form the World League to Free Women. Women are the jewels of the earth, and it's time they are treated as such.

Pains Present Past

Until the painful past becomes the past in you, it remains the painful present, which can get on your last nerve.

Peace-Hungry People

War is not good for peace, and peace is not good for war; peace doesn't create fear and intimidation like war. Peace must be created in the thoughts of the mind. Peace on earth and goodwill to all humanity. People are hungry and starving for peace as well as for food in their bellies. They need good water to drink, and a safe warm place to sleep. War affords none of these things.

The Gold Mine

Most people wish they had a gold mine so they could afford the nicer things in life. What they need is an FMO (a financial mental make-over). When people realize they are sitting on their "gold mind," they can have the "gold mine" and afford the nicer things in life. The gold is in our minds, but we must mine for it.

Thought Stream

We think of so many things every day, we can't possibly keep count of how many thoughts we are having, because even the thought of counting the present thought we are thinking constitutes another thought, which we would have to count. Therefore, it is best when I make an overview of my thoughts, which constitutes thinking about my thoughts, which leads to more thoughts about thoughts. It's all about our thoughts, that never-ending stream.

The Wet Dream

If at the end of the day we can only say, "I lived my life," instead of "I lived my dreams," then what a dry life we have lived. If a wet dream is better than a dry life, it's time to start living your dreams.

The Highs and the Lows

Of all the substances that can alter our state of mind, the two things that we can neither smoke, drink, pop, snort or inject, they are mind-altering poverty and mind-altering wealth.

Transmission of Success

Do not allow your thoughts to drive you. Instead drive your thoughts onto the road of success, steer your thoughts around the sharp curves of doubt, keep your mind lubricated with the oil of faith, ward off the corrosion of fear, keep hope alive, fuel those thoughts with high-octane persistence, and accelerate your progress toward your goal. In addition, remember to apply the brakes on any thought that gets in your way, and stop it! These things will keep the transmission of your own success running smoothly.

Three Good Things

If I asked you to quickly name three good things about yourself, what would you say, and what would your facial expression say? If you hesitated or could not think of anything, what does that tell you? Try this on yourself and others, and then think about it.

The Same Changed Thought

Though I've changed quiet a bit, I'm still the same. Though I'm still the same, I've changed quiet a bit.

Corrective Success

Having the ability to correct oneself is a key component on the road to success.

Valleys and Mountains

Where there are valleys, there must also be mountains. You can choose to live in the low valley of life, or you can choose to live on the highest mountain of life, but you cannot live in both places at the same time.

Believe in Yourself!

When you believe in yourself, you are like a mountain that will not be moved, like a light that continues to shine, like a wine that gets better with time. When you believe in yourself, latent abilities rise from your great storehouse within, talents and gifts emerge with confidence, and all obstacles are overcome effortlessly. Your life becomes a gentle, relaxing breeze filled with grace. When you believe in yourself, nothing seems too difficult to do or become. You become fluid with the ability to adapt into any shape. No situation that seems negative, or circumstance that spells doom, is greater than your faith in yourself! Love supports this faith in you, and love never fails; therefore, faith in yourself need not fail. Anxieties, fear, trepidation, and worry are mere ghosts, falseness attempting to keep you from manifesting your dreams, making the possible seem impossible. They are all lies. The truth is that when you believe in yourself, nothing real or unreal can change or take away your God-given faith and confidence in yourself!

The Strong, the Wise, the Weak

There is a saying that only the strong survive. How about adding that only the wise thrive, and the weak and unsuspecting hardly make it.

Fresh Thoughts for Sale

Perhaps we should shop for fresh thoughts as we shop for fresh produce. We would benefit greatly if we took the time to inspect our thoughts. If we have, rotten, wilted, expired or moldy thoughts, we need to toss them out of our minds. It is true that one bad apple can spoil the whole bushel. All negative thoughts have the same effect on our minds. This negativity shows up in our lives, as words, actions, and deeds. If it is not a fresh thought that adds freshness to your life, why think it? Toss it! And if you don't know what to think, pick up a copy of *Thoughts for A New Perspective.*

A Thought about Want

Stop wanting and start having.

Smile

Smile because it feels good!

Money People

Everybody wants the money, from paupers to presidents, children and the elderly; all over the world, everybody wants the money, from ancient times to the present, be they bankers or bums, coal miners or ministers, party planners or prostitutes. Millionaires want more millions, and billionaires want more billions. Today I have not seen a person turn down money. It has become a type of lifeblood to live on the earth, a seemingly true necessity. We have become money people.

Text Take Over

Imagine with me a text wedding. The minister texts, "Do you take her to be your beloved wife?" The groom with I phone in hand texts the words, "I do," sending it the minister and his fiance. She texts him a smile, "I love you," with her Android. Minister texts, "Do you take him to be your beloved husband?" She texts, "I do."

He texts her a smile with "I love you." After all is text and done, the minister sends a text blast: "I pronounce you husband and wife; you may text the bride with a kiss." They text each other "xoxo." Will they consummate the marriage with text sex?

The Hunt

That which man hunts, hunts man ... death!

Self-Importance

I have come to figure that no "one" of themselves is important, but that every "one" is important.

True Leadership Thought

You always have to know how a person is thinking in order to help them to think, to know, to learn, and to understand.

Perceiving the World

The illusion runs deep in the mind, it touches everything that we see, touch, hear, smell, and taste. It is ever convincing us that all is real. As we perceive the world, we believe our mind. The earth is flat as it is round. We all are trying to interpret the world which we perceive.

Precious Life

We all should be a life guard who guards life and have a record life, not a record funeral.

Why Buy the Lie?

When people's minds have no substance, the system can offer nearly anything, (any thought), and the people will buy it. I saw this printed on a name-brand piece of clothing, "Chill-in' like a villain." A villain cannot have peace, for they are on the run or in prison, or dead. The thought is without substance, for it is without truth. What about "America runs on Dunkin' Donuts"? Have you talked to any serious runners lately? Or "The best part of waking up is Folgers in your cup." I'd say the best part of waking up is waking up. Check out the world again, and then check yourself!

Your Greatest Tool!

Every tool ever made for the advancement of humanity's endeavors was conceived in the mind, created by our hands. Our greatest tool is truly our mind; it must be recognized as such, then scrutinized as well as utilized, for this has revolutionized our development individually and collectively

Uncommon Sense

I saw this message on a bumper sticker: "Please spay or neuter your pets." I stopped and wondered why. Well, dogs and cats have no sense; they only follow the urge to mate, without thought of consequences of their actions. An alley cat does not reason, and neither does a stray dog. Kittens and puppies are born this way all the time. Perhaps we need bumper stickers for people that say, "Please spay or neuter yourself if you are acting like a dog or a cat."

For Your Benefit

Everything I say or do is for your benefit, not mine. My benefit is helping you benefit. This is the way to truly share your cake and eat it too.

Ask and Ye Shall Receive

Quite some years ago, I would frequent a certain restaurant. I would order my favorite dish with all the trimmings. After I had my fill and was handed the bill, I simply paid what was due and went about my way. After many delicious meals at this restaurant, the server asked me, "Excuse me, sir, why don't ever leave me a tip? Is there something wrong with the food or my service?" I was caught in the middle of my thoughts; my first thought was *I have paid the bill in full what more do I owe?* The other thought was, *She sure is bold.* Nonetheless, the spotlight was on me; my reply was awaited. I said, *No, the food and the service is fine.* She said, *I just wondered.* Ever since that day, I have left a tip for all who serve me. She did not become any richer from my tip, but I have become richer from hers.

I Like the Way She Walks

A compliment is simply an observation accompanied by one's opinion. This may sound wild, but I will give it to you for what it is. I was dining at a fine restaurant, in Fort Wayne, Indiana. The hostess that seated the guests was a woman who had a very cute walk; each time she passed by while seating other guest, I would notice her. I thought to myself, *My thought is pure, untainted with lust or motive. She walks that way all the time but she never sees herself from the back, she has no view unless I share mine.* Nevertheless, I declined to share the compliment with her, as I know some things are better left unsaid and kept in one's head.

Forget Me Not

I know you think you almost have it all together, but don't forget one thing! Me.

Success from A to Z

A = Any	H = higher	O = one	V = victory
B = body	I = increase	P = prospers	W = wins
C = confused	J = joy	Q = quitting	X = x-ray
D = doubts	K = kill	R = reach	Y = yourself
E = embrace	L = loser	S = search	Z = zealously.
F = faith	M = mentality	T = try	
G = go	N = no	U = understand	

Acceptance

May I offer you a compliment? Of course! You are splendid. Offer accepted!

A Birds View

One morning I decided to do an experiment while walking down a country road. I projected my spirit/soul/mind approximately one hundred feet into the sky above my body. I wanted to see what I looked like walking down a country road alone. We are not contained in this physical body as we have supposed we are something so magnificent if we can experience a birds eye view.

The Power of Influence

The people we call our friends and associates will leave their influence upon us, so choose your friends carefully and be aware of your associates.

Trading Places

When you see the old, forget not that they were once young, and when you see the young, forget not that they shall become the old. They are one and the same, simply trading places in the illusion of time and space.

Celebrate Life!

The celebration of life is greeting everyone with respect, dignity, and love. For what we all have in common is life on this side. Life is the great common denominator, the equalizer, the fair balance. No one has a greater life than another; we all have the same…life!

Visiting Hours

I would advise you to visit the living while they live or you will visit them when they no longer are. Time affords us the window of opportunity to make that visit, make that call. Life is our only opportunity to do anything.

The Road to No Where

There is no road to no where for all roads go somewhere even if the place it goes to is no where, it is some where we call no where.

Ending Perfection

When something is perfect it is completely well balanced, why upset perfect complete balance? However it has been my observation noticing people upsetting the balance of perfection with body piercing and tattoos. A young woman with a beautiful face pierces her eye brow; it becomes infected and leaves a scar, ending perfection. Or an ex wife's name tattooed on a mans neck ending his perfect neck. Or having extra difficulty getting employed because you can't hide all your tattoos.

The Pill Life

Have you noticed how many pills are on the market today? It makes you wonder how humanity has survived with ills without the pills. Is it just a coincidence that the letter "p" was used in front of the word *ill*? A marketing by association stares you right in the face. A pill for every ill. Yet you still aren't healed. They just offer you another pill.

Silence

The only time that silence can be is as long as you do not say it; the moment you say "silence," the silence is not. In the presence of perfect silence, one must think it with the mind only, for only then can silence exist.

Relief

There is a time when pain and weakness cause us to forget all the physical and material pleasures of life. It is at that time we seek only relief.

Lifetime

We should try to maximize, not minimize, our time on planet Earth. However, our choices often make the difference.

Thought Precedes Action

We do very little without thought. Thought precedes action. Thought is the potential to create a movement, an expression from an intangible realm to the realm of tangibility.

An Attribute

The only thing that still wants to be right when proven to be wrong is your ego's pride. However when you can be corrected, it is an attribute. When you are wrong it is an attribute to apologize. It is better to be corrected than to go on uncorrected, thinking you are right when you are wrong.

Replacing Bad Habits

Old bad habits can be hard to break; however, they break easiest when replaced with a good habit.

You Represent More than You

We all are a part of someone's family. When we act a fool, we bring shame on our family, because we are representatives for our parents. We can also excel and bring honor to our family.

Unbelievable

I have never seen anything like this in my life: spirits with souls walking around in bodies made of clay, earthen vessels that do not know they are spirits. Instead they think they are bodies with parts.

Think with Me!

Everything outside of us tells us that this is it, guess what it is. The rest is within us.

I

I hop, I jump, I spin, I run, I exclaim, I am alive!

Past, Present, Future

The ever-present now is a type of eternity moment that always is. Can you fathom that the past starts now, the present starts now, and the future starts now? Therefore, is it correct to say that the eternal now that exists outside of time and space constraints dictates there is only the now? And if the now is all there is, what is the now?

The Light Matters

Have you ever tried to write a letter in the dark you will find it to be interesting when you turn on the light? Try reading a book upside down. Now turn off the lights and read.

What a Deal

This guy at work told me he was getting older by the minute. I told him that's not bad unless you are not getting any wiser. He said if he was wiser, he would not be in the shape he's in now.

Money Problems

If money is not a problem in your mind, then money seems not to be a problem in your life.

Mind and Body

If you want to be healthy, eat healthy foods and exercise. If you want to have a healthier mind, begin exercising your mind with healthy thoughts.

Pipe Dreams

In the land of abandoned dreams, you will find the last thing a person gives up: hope.

Displacement

When there is education, ignorance is no more. Likewise, when there is love, hatred is no more. So much in life that brings change is displacement.

Stopping Negativity

In the world we find ourselves surrounded by all sorts of negativity. Someone has been murdered, robbed, slandered, gossiped about, kidnapped, and more. Though we cannot stop this negativity, we do not have to participate in it.

The Heavy Load

Walking like a soldier with a heavy load, he carries it. It is his duty, he is focused, and so he walks on like a soldier with a heavy load.

Cussing This and That!

When a person has a potty mouth, cursing and using all manner of obscene and profane language, it is an outlet for their dissatisfaction with life. They curse at others and even inanimate objects, tools that break, doors that stick, and engines that won't start. "Come on, you lazy b__ch!" Yet they who have obtained peace from within have found life to be more satisfying than to curse the things of this life.

The Better Man

So often we say that we are not the man or woman we once were, and that's okay, because self-improvement is the name of the game, leaving us to say, "I am better!" It's time to outdo ourselves!

Weakness and Strength

Men watch other men. They look for weakness, and if they find weakness, they will walk on you. Yet if they see your strength, they respect you and walk around you.

Viewing the Future

We all desire to see the future. However, we must first see the future that we desire. Getting what you desire is not as important as desiring what you get.

Can You Do It?

What makes something doable is the absence of doubt. Doubt neutralizes faith, while faith eliminates doubt. Therefore, anything and everything is doable when we learn, and once we learn that it is doable.

Ignorance versus Understanding

Ignorance exists when clarity of understanding is absent. In all thy getting get understanding When we do not get clarity of understanding we get a misunderstanding which is the equivalent of ignorance for we have missed the understanding and confusion abounds.

Here We Go Again

No matter what we do, everything is getting closer. When women put on their makeup the time is getting closer to removing the same makeup. The moment we awake from our sleep, we are getting closer to going back to sleep. As soon as we are feeling full from eating, we are on our way to becoming hungry again. This is all we know, as though we were on a merry-go-round. We start out with no teeth and need twenty-four-hour care, and in our advanced age we are there again. "Once a man twice a child."

We Can Stop It!

If we stop killing, the killing will stop! The will to stop killing will stop it!

Lies, Lies, Lies

Our government lies, the evil lies, our parents lie, our religions lie, and we lie. But God is truth, and truth cannot and will not lie; it will stand. You cannot stand a lie; it is not the truth; therefore, it cannot stand but can only lie. You can stand the truth, for the truth will always stand.

Step into Greatness

Oftentimes when you step up, you will find that others step in and support your step into greatness.

So Shall It Be

Some will say that they would rather have money than love, and others will say life is a bitch and then you die. And this is their truth. So shall it be.

Stop the Bullshit

Bulls don't bullshit; people do. And when they have to eat their own bullshit, they say, "This bullshit is bullshit." But it's not the bull's shit; it's theirs.

The Golden Life

I see so many people selling their gold. I am wearing mine and living my life like it's golden: golden qualities, golden thoughts, never fading, always shining—full of precious value is the gold in life. I am golden light.

Sperm

When the race for life began, we swam faster than all the others. If we didn't, we would not be here today.

A Release on Life

I release by letting go of all the negative feelings that came from my hurtful, angry, or frightening thoughts about what did or did not happen, from all the things that overwhelmed me. And I invite the opposite to abide within me, because my freedom and happiness are important.

Working People

The reasons I don't talk about people at work are that there is nothing to talk about, and they're working people.

Ladder Thought

Remember, if you express things at the lowest rung in your mind and speech, you can always climb higher.

Medicine or Medi-Sin

I remember an old cowboy-and-Indian movie in which the Indians said, "White man medicine make red man sick." Today there is FDA-approved medicine that can make you very sick. They call them side effects of hopefully making you better, even if it kills you. Here are a few: stroke, heart failure, acting on dangerous impulses, new or worsening anxiety or depression, blindness, low blood pressure, high blood pressure, headaches, risk of suicide, abnormal bleeding, dizziness, diarrhea, insomnia, fainting, seizures, coma, difficulty breathing, decreased sex drive, birth defects, nausea, constipation, irritability, hallucinations, vomiting, liver or kidney damage, and death. There is something wrong with our medicine. Perhaps the Indians were right all along.

In the Beginning There Is No End

In the beginning of my writing, I realized that there would be no end, because thought seems to beget thought. Nevertheless, it has been a pleasure having you alongside me on this epic journey of *Thoughts for a New Perspective*. May it cause you to think like you have never thought before. And act from the noblest of thoughts that you can think, give them expression, and it will cause a shift in consciousness. May the good thoughts planted in the fertile garden of your mind bear much fruit and be shared with others.